A CERTAIN RISK

LIVING YOUR FAITH AT THE EDGE

PAUL RICHARDSON

ZONDERVAN®

ZONDERVAN.com/
AUTHORTRACKER
follow your favorite authors

ZONDERVAN

A Certain Risk
Copyright © 2010 by Paul Andrew Richardson

This title is also available as a Zondervan ebook. Visit www.zondervan.com/ebooks.

This title is also available in a Zondervan audio edition. Visit www.zondervan.fm.

Requests for information should be addressed to:

Zondervan, Grand Rapids, Michigan 49530

Library of Congress Cataloging-in-Publication Data

Richardson, Paul, 1967-.
    A certain risk : living your faith at the edge / Paul Richardson.
        p. cm.
    Includes bibliographical references and index [if applicable].
    ISBN 978-0-310-29132-9
    1. Christian life. 2. Risk-taking (Psychology)—Religious aspects—Christianity.
    3. Richardson, Paul, 1967-. I. Title.
    BV4598.15.R53 2009
    248.4—dc22   20090041489

All Scripture quotations, unless otherwise indicated, are taken from the Holy Bible, *New International Version®, NIV®*. Copyright © 1973, 1978, 1984 by Biblica, Inc.™ Used by permission of Zondervan. All rights reserved worldwide. Other versions used include: the New American Standard Bible (NASB). © Copyright 1960, 1962, 1963, 1968, 1971, 1972, 1973, 1975, 1977, 1995 by The Lockman Foundation; the New King James Version (NKJV). Copyright © 1982 by Thomas Nelson, Inc. Used by permission. All rights reserved; and the King James Version (KJV).

Any Internet addresses (websites, blogs, etc.) and telephone numbers printed in this book are offered as a resource. They are not intended in any way to be or imply an endorsement by Zondervan, nor does Zondervan vouch for the content of these sites and numbers for the life of this book.

Cover design: John Hamilton Design
Cover photo: Gaylon Wampler
Interior design: Cindy LaBreacht

Printed in the United States of America

09 10 11 12 13 14 • 20 19 18 17 16 15 14 13 12 11 10 9 8 7 6 5 4 3 2 1

TO MY GREATEST HERO —
MY FATHER

CONTENTS

FOREWORD BY
ERWIN RAPHAEL MCMANUS

I remember when I first met Paul. Actually I knew of him long before we finally met face-to-face. I had recently become the new senior pastor of what is now known as Mosaic, and it can not be overstated how badly the transition was going. I faced opposition and conflict at every turn. I must confess that while I knew transitions are always challenging, I wasn't prepared for what was to come. I thought people would welcome a shift in ethos from standardization to innovation and from conformity to creativity. When my brother saw what I was attempting to do, he cautioned that not everyone shares my preference of decentralization — some people want the comfort of a world that is orderly and a system that is highly centralized and tightly controlled. Clearly, I didn't listen well.

One night there was an emergency meeting in our living room. It was to help the few twenty-somethings at the church who were struggling with the transition. I quickly discovered that the church's culture was a filter for late adopters of every age and generation.

In the midst of this, I kept hearing about Paul. "Wait till Paul gets back." Evidently he was somewhere in Asia, changing the world as he is prone to do. "Let's see what Paul has to say about all this." Whoever Paul was, he had the absolute trust and respect of everyone who knew him.

In walks this kid in his early twenties with movie-star good looks, the poise of a Tibetan monk, and the character of Jesus. He almost never spoke, but you knew he was listening. Silence seemed his preferred state of being and the limelight his greatest enemy.

But when he spoke ...

It was as if I had been transported back to the times of Jonah or Amos or, maybe more on point, Hosea. He spoke with the power of love, with strength of character, and with genuine humility. Even then he was intent on pursuing with every fiber of his being all that God would ask of him to make tangible God's love for humanity. Paul was there to serve.

I came to love Paul Richardson that day.

Yes, any other word or explanation is inadequate. Few travel together in such a way, where geography is incidental to walking side by side.

Nearly twenty years ago I began a crusade that has been summarized in Mosaic's fifth core value: Creativity Is the Natural Result of Spirituality. I felt the modern movement of the Christian faith had abandoned, if not betrayed, the creative essence of the human spirit. *Creativity* was a profane and sacrilegious term. To imply that humans were designed with creative potential and that God intends for us to be a part of the creative process was nowhere near being in vogue. Like Sacraments reserved for priests to dispense, creativity was God's alone, and he did not intend to share.

I have been told more than once that people are simply not creative, that what they need is a task to keep them busy. Others have argued that only God is creative and he shares his glory with no one. Still others insist that discipline is what makes a disciple, not freedom. It seems to me the purpose of a disciple is to bring freedom: when we are conformed to the character of Christ we become our most unique selves. Soon I was on a mission to make the language of the creative spirit the common vernacular of faith. I felt that this was the hill I was supposed to die on—life is a creative act.

Since the day I met Paul, I have never stood on that hill alone. Paul is an apostle of the creative spirit.

This is why this book is so important. Paul is a throwback to the days when people wrote out of their life experience and not their research. He is an adventurer and a pioneer. He is a creative and an activist. He is a reflective thinker and a practical doer. He is both artist and agent—bringing beauty and change to the world.

Here in this work he provides not only the creative spark to inspire you but the burning fire that very well may consume you.

I have walked with Paul, and it has changed my life. I invite you to journey with him through the pages ahead and discover how my friend and hero changes you.

dream - risk - create,

erwin raphael mcmanus

FOUNDER: McManus Studios
EXPLORER: The Awaken Group
LEAD PASTOR: Mosaic

Living Your Faith

at the Edge

Take a globe and locate the continent of Australia. Then drag your finger north across the Great Barrier Reef and turn slightly to the left. There you will see a string of tropical islands stretched across the equator. These islands comprise Indonesia, the fourth-most-heavily-populated nation on earth. The son of missionaries, I was raised in a village carved out of the remote jungle on one of these islands. My earliest memories are of sitting on the laps of warriors, eating sago grubs in a thatch-roofed, smoke-filled man-house. While my dad translated the Bible into the local language and my mom treated patients in her medical clinic, I ran barefoot through the jungle, chasing egrets with a bow and arrow. Eventually our family relocated to Southern California. I came of age trying to figure out what it means to be civilized. Meanwhile, a relentless love for the "Islands of Fire" never ceased to pulse in my bloodstream. At thirty-one I returned with my wife, Cyndi, and our two children, Katie and Josiah. Our son Stephen was born here.

Our city is cradled in a valley between three living volcanoes. At any given time, we can look to the horizon and see thousands of tons of ash being launched into the sky. The ash is caught by the ocean breeze and drifts back to earth, creating some of the most fertile soil on the planet. Tantalizingly green rice paddies carpet the towering slopes of our mountains. Indonesian highlands grow some of the most aromatic coffee on earth. But by far the most beautiful part of this country is her people. Indonesians are warm and friendly. They live with a blended diversity of colorful cultures, and they are astoundingly creative. Some Indonesians also suffer pervasively. Our family is doing all we can to foster a movement of freedom for the oppressed. We work with a network of more than thirty orphanages, youth centers, Christian schools, and other adventures into the soul of Indonesia's future.

When I brought my family from California to the islands of my birth about ten years ago, I came with the intention to reveal God to others. God brought me here to reveal his heart to me. How could I have known that throughout our years here, God would so intimately and gently lead us by the hand? After walking with God for a while, people begin to pick up on what he enjoys. What do you enjoy? I revel in friendships that grow deeper through the years. I get high on improvisational road trips. There's nothing quite like carving into a freshly chopped coconut with a spoon. Cyndi prefers to sip tea in the morning, and I go for coffee. We both love Indian curry and relish Thai food.

I don't know what kind of food God likes, but I know that he enjoys faith. From God's perspective, faith emits the sweetest, most beautiful aroma in all of his creation. This book is about faith. You won't be reading about an intellectual sort of faith so much as a faith that reveals itself through attitudes, decisions, movements, and actions. This kind of faith doesn't necessarily draw us to places like Africa and Asia, but it always carries us beyond ourselves. This book is centered in the awakening of faith, when the chains and barriers that paralyze a person are broken and that person rises up in response to the Spirit of God and is set free to breathe God's life into our world. It's what I call "faith at the edge."

Faith at the edge. These four words remind me of the day my college roommate, Eric, and I were about to explore a sunken warship that lies off the coast of Bali. I had pored over a book about scuba diving and sailed through a written test. I was able to quote the rules of diving and had memorized the hand signals to communicate under water. Now I faced only one slight problem. I'd never actually worn scuba gear. I stared down into the choppy ocean and regretted my decision to try this. The deep looked up at me and opened its giant mouth, as if poised to eat me for lunch. Someone behind me was telling me to step over the edge.

Scuba diving involves three actions that logically do not belong together: hoisting an enormous metal tank onto your back, strapping it around your body, and plunging into a watery abyss. Not wanting to reveal to the others how terrified I had suddenly become, I jumped. As I sank into the depths, my soul was jolted by a surge of fear, followed by a desperate craving for the surface. I felt as if I were chained to a millstone. Glancing up, I noticed the sky sinking away. I thought, *I don't want to die just yet.* In a primal state of panic, I actually considered unbuckling myself from the apparatus. *No, wait.* I had to trust the book. The book said, "Never stop breathing!"

I realized that I was breathing after all. This wasn't so bad. I was floating, suspended effortlessly in a wide-open space. All the days of my life, I had been bound to the ceiling of the water. Now, though, I was free to experience what it really means to swim. This was swimming beyond the edge. Here, on the far side of fear, was a freedom I had never dreamed possible—a freedom to go deeper and closer to the captivating underwater beauty that had previously existed only in aquariums and on television.

Like diving, faith is initially counterintuitive. It defies human nature, which is why it is associated with risk. Diving into God is dangerous simply because his dreams for us are worth giving our lives for. Instead of taking this jump, many of us won't go anywhere near the edge. In fact, we tend to cling to the surface. The only faith we have known is something like swimming in one of those round plastic pools we sometimes see in a neighbor's yard. This is the version of faith that occasionally flutters into our thoughts on Sunday mornings or when we remember to say the blessing over a meal. It doesn't have much to do with Monday mornings, and it tends to evaporate under pressure. I know all about that. I've confused faith with abstract theoretical preferences. I know what it means to be driven by guilt and to work myself to the bone for God's approval. I've died a slow death from trying to figure out and follow all the rules. None of these have anything to do with the faith God is holding out for us. God calls us to something so much deeper—a faith that sets us free to be guided by his voice, to see our world with his eyes and respond with the passions of his heart.

God is moving across the earth in search of men and women who will dare to take the leap of faith. He is offering us the chance to rise up and actuate his dreams for our generation. You and I were born into days of adversity stirred together with unprecedented opportunity. The signs are everywhere. Our times distinguish individuals who live their faith at the edge from those who shrink back. Does your soul cry out for a faith that sets you free to voyage into the depths of God's dreams? Do you crave a faith that drenches you with hope and breaks open the floodgates of God's movements through you? The words on the pages ahead are written for you. Will you stare down a certain risk and take the jump?

Who knows?

God might be waiting on the other side.

When the Son of Man comes,

will he find faith on the earth?

JESUS

CHAPTER 1

RESPOND

TRIANGULATING FAITH

In response to the dawn peeking over the eastern mountains, roosters cleared their throats and began to cackle at one another, touching off the familiar routine. In the half light, bleary-eyed fishermen hauled boats ashore, then wearily scrubbed their nets after a night of working in the open sea. Mothers began to boil water for rice. Men stood from their morning prayers and reached for their first cups of steaming *kopi Aceh*. Children yawned and stretched on their rattan sleeping mats, delighted to be waking up on a Sunday, the one day of the week that Indonesian schools are closed. By 7:00 a.m., athletes were eagerly gathering to compete in a citywide field day. Minutes later, the grass they were standing on would be strewn with more than five thousand corpses.

The earthquake struck with a furious jolt. A 9.3 blitzkrieg of thundering chaos, it rocked northern Sumatra, Indonesia, for eight minutes. The cacophony of collapsing walls and shattering glass drowned out the thousands of screaming voices. Untold thousands had been crushed in their own bedrooms and kitchens.

But the worst was still to come.

The sound was unearthly. Later, many would say they thought two oncoming trains were colliding. Three towering waves bulldozed the city, obliterating everything in their paths. Schools and bridges exploded. Palm trees snapped like twigs. Houses were forced from their foundations and carried away in a million churning, broken parts. In agonizing moments of decision repeated countless times across the disaster zone, mothers and fathers selected which of their children to pick up as they ran for the hills.

On that horrible morning, December 26, 2004, 283,000 people were swept into eternity, while double that number were instantly left without food, shelter, or clean water. The tsunami was one of the deadliest natural disasters to ever assault humanity. For hundreds of miles along the Sumatran coastline, villages, streets, coffee plantations, markets, and hospitals were annihilated. The survivors staggered to the edges of hastily dug pits, where they dropped the mangled bodies of their dead children, parents, neighbors, and friends. Within weeks, the survivors were gathered into sprawling, muddy Internally Displaced Persons (IDP) camps.

Two months later, I arrived in the city of Banda Aceh. The condition on the ground was far more catastrophic than I had imagined. I felt like I'd landed on another planet. My stomach tightened as I stared in disbelief at wreckage that stretched to the horizon.

My reason for coming was to launch the rebuilding of a school. After surveying the chaos, I realized that the school would have to wait. I joined with a relief team that had identified a dozen IDP camps clustered around the city. Our purpose was to carry in critical supplies and provide medical care and counseling for the grieving. A nightmarish fog of terrifying memories hung over these camps day and night. Two months after the tsunami, men, women, and children stared at the world with remote storm clouds in their bloodshot eyes.

One night I was lying on my sleeping mat at our command center. The odor of death in the humid air was suffocating—hundreds of rotting corpses were still being pulled out of the mud every day. I was exhausted. Yet much worse than my physical discomfort were the repeated images of vacant, hopeless eyes. When I closed my eyes, I saw theirs. Every person I met had lost someone.

Earlier that day, one woman had told me in fluent English that she had been a professor in Banda Aceh. She had received her doctorate from an American university. Her husband was now dead and her two small children had been swept away. One of them had been discovered face down in the mud, and the other was never found. She was alone in a sea of strangers, languishing beneath the heavy sky for two months. She had no plan and no idea what to do next. In the great journey from birth to death, she and thousands like her were cruelly and viciously sidelined. As I thought about her, my heart cried out to God, *Where are you in all of this? I feel so incapable of responding to these heartbroken people. They so desperately need you. Give me something to say. Oh, Lord Jesus, touch me with your words of life to speak to them.*

The Spirit waited, leaving me suspended in the angst of my soul. Then he whispered, *You cannot hear what I want you to say until I show you what I see. Fix your eyes on what is unseen.* In that moment I pressed my eyes shut. Before me were beautiful souls with infinite value. They were the Creator's masterpiece. Each was deeply treasured and eternally loved. Yet their world had roared, puncturing their souls and pressing the life out of them. Harassed and helpless, trapped between life and death, they were paralyzed and imprisoned by powers more devastating than any ocean wave.

A new realization began to form in my heart. Dozens of relief agencies were carrying rice, water, and blankets to the survivors. The construction of bridges, businesses, and hospitals was underway. These efforts were crucial, yet beyond the immediate needs in this catastrophic situation were even more salient necessities. Each survivor must do more than survive — each must discover the faith to rise up through his gripping inner paralysis and begin to forge a new future. A glimmer of hope must somehow emerge from the twisted, rotting mess of wreckage. The resurgence of every street, village, and town depended on it. The people's lives hinged upon it. The survival of their culture demanded it. *What could I do?* I lay in the darkness, feeling overwhelmed by these thoughts. I tried to close them out of my mind and finally drifted into a restless sleep.

The next morning our group hauled relief supplies to another IDP camp. Now terrified of the sea, these survivors had fled into the mountains south of Banda Aceh. Taking notice of a group of elders sitting together, I approached and asked if I could join them. They politely made room for me. After a few minutes of small talk, several of the men shared their stories, vividly describing tragic losses during the tsunami. As they talked, others sat quietly, staring at nothing in particular.

Seeing their eyes, I wondered what might happen if I spoke about the future. Was I overstepping my bounds? I decided to run the risk. After quietly praying, I began to speak, slowly at first. Having expressed my sorrow for their loss, I said, "People all over the world are praying for you." Then I wondered aloud, "Does God have another future waiting for you?" Looking at their faces, God's love began overwhelming my heart and shaping my words. "From out of all the thousands of people who were lost, God chose to keep you and these others alive one more day. That must mean that he has a purpose for each of you."

They began to lean forward. Something about my words had caught their attention. I continued, "Will you lead your people again?" Several men lifted their heads. The invitation to respond had fanned the embers of life in their tired eyes. I pressed forward: "Those little children playing over there are waiting for you to stand up and take action. They need you to look into their eyes and call them into their future. I believe God is offering you the chance to help the next generation grow up to become men and women of strength and courage. Imagine what might happen if they saw you creating, working, rebuilding your lives, and offering them a new hope."

To my amazement, not a single man reacted by saying, "How could *you* possibly know what we've been through?" Instead, they drank in the challenge. It seemed that their hearts were already primed to rise up and rebuild their lives. All they had needed was a voice to call them over the tipping point into action. They began to interact in the early light of new possibilities. Imaginations stirred. Within minutes they had reoriented themselves to a radically new mindset. Excitement rose into their voices. Ideas flew. What would happen if the entire community worked together to help one family, then another, then another? Eventually I was no longer a part of the conversation. Over the next few hours, I listened with astonishment as they wrenched themselves free from the chains of mental paralysis and activated the creative process.

Soon they were outlining their plan of action. Their strategy was to gather all of the able men, return to their destroyed communities, and rebuild together, starting with whatever materials they could pull from the wreckage. They would all work together to serve one. By a roll of dice, they would select the second family, then the third. Purpose had emerged from lassitude. By choosing to activate solutions in response to the urgent problems around them, they were creating—creating life and hope out of death and despair.

Responders were being set free.

RESPONSIVENESS ∽

No conversation has ever affected me so deeply. To this day, the stark contrast between humanity reduced and humanity rising is etched in my mind. Returning from Sumatra to my home in eastern Indonesia, I began to see the parallels in my own life. I realized that in numerous ways I am the one who is internally displaced. Be assured, I am not equating anything I've been through to the horrific agony tsunami survivors have endured. In comparison, the waves that tend to reduce me are more like tiny ripples on the surface of a pond. Perhaps this is why the responsiveness of that small group of elders left such an unforgettable impression on me. This impression eventually became the spur that caused me to begin writing.

My own life is the setting for this book. I apologize for this, but I just don't see any other way to approach a subject like faith.

I would be irresponsible to write about awakening into God with a cold detachment, as if I were a biologist dissecting a dead frog in a laboratory or a researcher analyzing a survey. Even now, the words on the pages ahead are being dragged through the battleground of my soul. This battleground is strewn with defeat and marked by victory. I am determined not to be ashamed of either.

When I began to write, I was personally challenged by painstaking questions. If individuals who lost everything can rise up and create after a tsunami, what prevents me from responding to a critical statement with a genuine expression of kindness? If they can rebuild a city, can I rebuild a stranded relationship? Does adversity tend to wash over me, reducing me to a mere shadow of the life God created me to live? Am I a responsive husband and father? When I come across antagonistic individuals or people who are noticeably different from me, how do I respond? Do I tend to shrink away into my own made-up, vicarious universe?

Is God's Spirit alive in me? Does his Word empower me, forging a Spirit-filled response to others? Am I borne along by an activated faith that lifts me into God's heart and propels me forward as a joyful responder to the world he loves? Is my soul rooted in the One "who so loved the world," a world stranded in spiritual, mental, physical, and emotional isolation and powerlessness, that he gave his life in response?

Taking a good, hard look in the mirror is healthy for anyone's soul. But there was something else that I needed to answer. Am I fated to stay the way I am, or is it possible for me to change, to become a man who gathers the raw materials of adversity and creates eternal works of art in the world around me? This is not an easy question, but I am persuaded that, yes, you and I can move from internal paralysis to becoming responders. The apostle John phrased it this way: "Everyone born of God overcomes the world."[1] Certain individuals around me are living evidence of John's audacious statement. Take my grandmother, for example. What person driving down the street would ever have guessed that the elderly woman limping along with a cane toward church on Sunday mornings was a creative prodigy?

Throughout her ninety-three years, my grandmother never would have dreamed of acting in a drama, playing a piano, or even singing in her church choir. I don't ever remember seeing her with a paintbrush. We all had a big laugh at the confused look on her face when she asked sheepishly, "Why do computers come with mice?" Ah, but how she exuded creativity in response to everything life threw in her face. Her responsiveness to other people always began by drawing from the hope that bloomed deep within her. Whether she was fixing Yorkshire pudding for a homeless mother or caring for a friend in the hospital, she always seemed to paint her world with the purest expressions.

The most remarkable thing about my grandmother is that she suffered immensely. Her unrelenting abundance of hope defied logic. If anyone had the right to slither away into cynicism and bitterness, she did. My grandfather came home from soldiering in the Second World War, moved the family from her beloved Prince Edward Island to faraway British Columbia, where they knew almost no one, then died of cancer, leaving her alone with their four boys, little money, and no income. She responded by sinking every last penny into opening a restaurant near the Victoria harbor. She continued to raise her sons alone. The miracle of her humble life was the sublime contrast between her circumstances and her staggering fortitude of hope. Somehow, she gathered the raw materials of adversity and used them to create hope in the hearts around her. The art of her life was painted as the brilliant, more radiant primary colors of hope rose out to overpower and even replace the darker, more oppressive colors of grief.

People like her are rare, but when we find them, we want to drink them up like a refreshing glass of cool water on a hot summer day. We want to stay close to them, to let the hope in their souls irrigate us. They are all the evidence I need that God is pervasively at work throughout his creation. He is whispering, creating, redeeming, orchestrating, and drawing all of humanity to himself.[2] God is calling us to rise into the paths he has marked out for us. Some are responsive. They see God everywhere, hear his voice, and taste the love for the world that burns in his heart. They intimately know the warmth of God's voice, thrive in the beauty of his dreams and see his purposes being worked out in all circumstances. Others are unresponsive. The difference is found in one word. This word gets tossed around in sermons, but at the office it's a bit more difficult to dig up. Jesus was astonished when he met people who lived with it.

This word is *faith*.

Faith is often defined as a mental affirmation that God is what the Bible says he is and that all the stories about Jesus are true and so on. I believe that the faith Jesus was so enamored with is something much deeper than that. Our mental affirmations about God are *symptoms* of faith, but they are not faith itself. What is faith? Faith is an intimate and responsive relationship with reality. I realize that faith is not typically defined this way. After all, what am I, some kind of a Buddhist? What could I possibly mean that faith is an intimate and responsive relationship with reality? Reality is, well ... reality is *real*. Faith is all about believing in God, right?

Ah, but can you see the problem?

Jesus described calloused hearts as "ever hearing but never understanding ... ever seeing but never perceiving."[3] Perhaps the easiest way to understand faith is to identify what it is not. Those who lack faith tend to compartmentalize reality, mentally tearing apart the elements of reality and stuffing them into separate chambers as if they have nothing to do with each other. We see this compartmentalization running rampant in society. The objects and people we cherish are naturally given the places of honor. Everyone else is rounded up and crammed into another chamber. Joy and laughter live in the den. An addiction might be shoved under the bed. Other secrets are stuffed into a closet. Hurting and lonely people rent space in the garage. Our own sour attitude sits impatiently in the car waiting for the ride to church. The glory of God politely greets us as we pull into the church parking lot. God tends to be held at a distance and walled away from the rest of life. Everything is disjointed.

FUSION ∽

God prefers wide-open spaces and the sound of wind stirring tall grass and rustling through leaves. Jesus said, "The wind blows wherever it pleases."[4] No corner of our lives can really be hidden from God. Truth waits for the moment we open our eyes to the convergence of God and Monday morning. Catching a glimpse of God in the mundane is the dawning of faith. Faith is the certainty of God's presence near the water cooler and the evidence that he is sitting at the staff meeting. Faith is experiencing all of life in the fusion of heaven and earth.

The apostle Paul told a group of philosophers, "For in him we live and move and have our being."[5] What does it mean to live and move and have our being in God? God is love, and we are called to live and move and have our being in his love. God is a communicator, and we are called to live and move and have our being in the sound of his voice. God initiates and calls. We are caused and called. God pours out his grace, and faith opens up our souls and lets his grace rain on us. God dreams to redeem our circumstances, and faith sets us free to respond to his dreams. God is engaged with the world 365 degrees around us, and faith awakens and unleashes our responsiveness to his engagement.

My wife, Cyndi, lives in this fusion. She listens to God's voice throughout the day. As I walk together with her, it is obvious that she is involved with God and he is involved with her. Cyndi's faith is growing and thriving. She can't wait to sit with God in the morning. She goes to sleep with his words on her mind. Her faith leaves God's fingerprints all over my life. In the evenings she responds to God by pouring her soul through her piano and creating beautiful music that draws my own heart into worship.

Think about the following words from King David's personal journal. As you read what he wrote, imagine yourself grabbing a pen and originating them. Be an insider. Climb into them and look around, as if you are the one jotting them down during your coffee break or typing them into a Facebook entry. Don't let yourself compartmentalize them, storing them in an abstract place that has no relevance to your actual life. Imagine them portraying how you perceive yourself at your job or shaping your response to a seemingly impossible situation you are facing today.

> *You are my lamp, O LORD;*
>> *the LORD turns my darkness into light.*
> *With your help I can advance against a troop;*
>> *with my God I can scale a wall*
>
> *It is God who arms me with strength*
>> *and makes my way perfect.*
> *He makes my feet like the feet of a deer;*
>> *he enables me to stand on the heights.*
> *He trains my hands for battle;*
>> *my arms can bend a bow of bronze.*
> *You give me your shield of victory;*
>> *you stoop down to make me great.*
> *You broaden the path beneath me,*
>> *so that my ankles do not turn.*[6]

David lived and moved and had his being in God. God was his strength, his vision, and his protector, right down to his ankles. Only in this fusion, which the Bible calls faith, is our responsiveness to God, to others, and to our circumstances awakened. God wants to blow through all of your life and breathe on everything in you and around you. He wants you to see him at work in the details. Ready yourself. He will tear down your walls and rattle your windows until you know him, see him, and hear him *everywhere*.

TUMBLING WALLS ∽

How does God tear down our walls? Perhaps for others he gently and patiently dismantles their walls brick by brick. For stubborn and unresponsive wall builders like me, he resorts to extreme measures. At some point in every wall builder's life, cold winds begin to stir up the waters around us. Devastating waves rise and roll, and as they swamp our compartments, fear invades our souls. Fervently bailing water, we find ourselves crashing onto jagged rocks. Our compartments of safety splinter into a thousand pieces, and we tumble into the depths. We cry out for our Creator, and in desperation we cling to his promises and wait to see if he really is God when and where it counts.

I suspect that David's ability to see God everywhere around him is related to the words he wrote *before* the passage we just examined.

> *The waves of death swirled about me;*
> *the torrents of destruction overwhelmed me.*
> *The cords of the grave coiled around me;*
> *the snares of death confronted me.*
> *In my distress I called to the LORD;*
> *I called out to my God.*
> *From his temple he heard my voice;*
> *my cry came to his ears.* [7]

Initially, David envisions God as sitting in a faraway temple. Then David describes his moment of fusion. He writes with breathtaking imagery, portraying the Almighty as parting the heavens and thundering into his personal crisis. [8]

My own family once endured our own waves of desperation. For three days those waves carved horrifying and holy memories into our souls. We were suddenly the ones stranded in miry clay, crying out for mercy. In the ferocious wind, God reached out and grasped our hands and lifted us up from the waves. His voice was clear, and his grip was strong. The method of God's response hammered a mighty blow against my walls—walls that had blinded me to the intimate awareness that God is moving from within every moment and circumstance.

First, a little background: More than five years before the tsunami rolled over the western shores of Indonesia, I was recruited to become the principal of a Christian international school there. The recruiter did his job well. Knowing that I had been born and raised in Indonesia, and that my professional background was in educational leadership, he described the position in a way that immediately jumped out at me. We'd get the chance to be a witness for Christ among expatriate families from all over the world. Seeds planted in the hearts of those students would eventually grow and multiply in dozens of countries. The city where I'd be working was ripe for new ministries with college students. Then there were the side perks. The recruiter assured me that my family would be living in a breezy mountain city where the altitude took the edge off the heat. That sounded fun! To live in Indonesia is to live near the beach and to enjoy the beauty of creation. One can drink freshly squeezed sirsak juice or bite into a limitless supply of the biggest, juiciest mangoes imaginable.

With images of swaying palm trees dancing in my imagination, I started getting excited about a possible new chapter in our lives. Because the position at the school offered no salary, it was a premium chance for God to reveal whether this really was his chosen path for us. We began to spread the news about the opportunity. Six months later, God had gathered several churches and a small yet remarkably generous tribe of prayer warriors and supporters for us to make the move. After giving away almost everything we owned, we felt we were ready.

This brings me to the twelfth of August, 1999, the day that we were supposed to drive to the airport and fly to Indonesia. That morning dawned with a splendid California sunrise. After enjoying the Creator's handiwork in the eastern sky, I swam some laps in the pool of the house where we were staying. After a hot shower, I left the outside door standing open to release the steam. Cyndi and I began to sort through our suitcases as we readied our family to drive to the airport.

Sometime later that morning Cyndi asked, "Where's Josiah?" Now, all these years later, I still hear my wife's voice calling out for our nine-month-old son, who had days before learned to crawl. *Where have you crawled off to, buddy?* After searching for a few minutes around the house, we started to get worried. Then Cyndi noticed the open door. We rushed outside only to look down through ten feet of still, blue water to see him lying motionless in a fetal position over the pool drain. I plunged into the water and gathered my son's cold, lifeless body into my arms. It wasn't until I had started swimming toward the surface did I begin to grasp that something was terribly wrong. Josiah was the temperature of death. Not until my face emerged from the water and my ears heard a mother's scream did it fully dawn on me that our son had drowned.

The rest of the morning is somewhat of a blur in my mind, but there is one part I will never forget. I collapsed to my knees onto the forest green carpet as my brother Shannon tried to breathe oxygen into Josiah's water-saturated lungs. There in that horrible moment, I lifted my hands to heaven, and my soul cried out to Yahweh. It was the cry of a father who had lost his son. There is no combination of words in the English language that adequately describes the desperation of that moment. Up until then, I reckoned that I knew God, but I had never truly experienced the fullest intimacy with him. All of my prayers before and since then, gathered together into one gigantic heap, still do not add up to that moment.

Since then, I have so deeply craved to remember who I saw that morning, to see the universe in his eyes and feel the warmth of his presence once again. Being near him was like coming in from a blizzard and warming my hands near the fire. He slowly stood and moved toward me. I remember thinking he was moving too slowly. I urgently wanted him to move faster, to hurry and rescue my son. Instead, he gathered me up into his arms, and, for the first time in my life, I breathed. To this day I have been like a broken and trembling addict, longing to know that same rest just once again. Perhaps I will have to wait until my soul is swallowed up by eternal life. There, resting in that timeless moment, I saw the face of a Father who had watched his only son crucified. It wasn't until the firefighters arrived that I came back up out of my vision. Or was it a hallucination generated by trauma? Perhaps psychologists have a term for what I experienced. All I know is that since that moment I haven't been the same person.

Meanwhile, breath after breath, minute after minute, my brother had refused to give up on his little nephew. At one point Shannon noticed Josiah take a breath on his own. He would later describe it as a hiccup. That one tiny breath reignited a glimmer of hope for his survival. The firefighters rushed Josiah and me to a helicopter, which lifted us into the sky and carried us over the city of angels to Children's Hospital.

Hours later, Cyndi and I were witnesses to our son connected to a tangle of various wires and hoses, and we were told something about his brain not responding to a test. He had experienced a series of severe brain seizures. A doctor told us it would take "divine intervention" for him to live. Even if he did live, he would have permanent brain damage. We were so low. Our bodies were standing upright, yet our souls were crumpled on the floor. If it weren't for our two-year-old Katie, we would have laid down next to Josiah's little body in the ICU, curled him into our arms, and slipped into the darkness with him.

Then hope arrived.

God pulled his car into the parking garage, walked through the front door of the hospital, entered the elevator, and came up to the ICU waiting room. Our church bulletin is printed with the words *Mosaic: A Community of Faith, Hope, and Love.* On this morning, those familiar old words sprang from the paper and leapt into our lives. They started to arrive at the hospital in ones and twos until there were more than one hundred. Standing in our tempest with us, God's own body filled up the waiting room and flowed into the hallway. I still remember their faces. They were a united expression of hope, an improvisational phalanx of prayer warriors called into action. With eyes that brimmed with courage, they offered their embraces.

Our family members flew in from the Midwest and the East Coast, arriving later that night. We were to learn later that many thousands of people all over the world had read about Josiah's plight over prayer networks and had paused to pray for him that day. Christ himself reached out through them, gathering us into his arms. He was breathing hope through his body, the church, into our moment of terror, confusion, and desperation.

Some brought food. One couple who lived nearby offered us their apartment. Others simply wept with us. All of them gathered into circles and prayed in the power of the Spirit. A few of our pastors and elders entered the ICU and placed their hands on Josiah. They prayed in the fusion of heaven and earth, with hearts that reflected an awareness that the Father was somehow going to reveal himself in this moment. For them, the hospital room was an altar. Standing around our son, they prayed with an assurance that God was already victorious in this event. Their words spoke of purpose for Josiah's life and hope that he would be raised up from a watery grave to glorify the name of Christ. As they prayed, the shadow of the Almighty hovered over his fragile, frail body and began to stir life. Movement was initially noticed in his feet. Then it slowly began to spread through his body until he opened his eyes and looked around. Josiah blinked. He seemed to be wondering where he was and why all these people were standing around him. On the third day, he was released from Children's Hospital by an amazed doctor who declared he had never seen such a complete and rapid recovery from a condition of such severity.

Just yesterday afternoon, Josiah dribbled a soccer ball toward me. He faked one direction, got me all turned around, then spun the other way and effortlessly rocketed a goal past me. As I picked myself up off the ground, I watched proudly as his teammates high-fived him. I will always call Josiah my champion. Many athletes face worthy opponents to gain the victor's trophy. How many of us can say that we have grappled with death and risen victoriously? Day after day of seeing him alive and filled with such joy reminds me of those who revealed God in the midst of our pain and desperation.

Josiah lives because a diverse group of people rose up and took action in response to a family's desperate need. My brother Shannon responded by immediately performing CPR. The firefighters responded by speeding to the scene and immediately calling for an airlift. The hospital staff responded by rushing Josiah into the emergency room and doing everything within their power to restore his life. Thousands of believers responded by praying. Over a hundred members of a church responded by going to the hospital. Pastors and elders responded by laying hands on a hopeless situation and becoming the conduits of God's healing touch.

To me these memories vividly portray what it means to call ourselves the Body of Christ. Through the responsiveness of men and women of faith, it was God who responded. Later I would grasp why, in my vision, our Father came to me in such a calm and relaxed manner. He was already stirring in the hearts of his children, calling them to rise up, to voice his words, and to become his own hands and feet. If only I could build some sort of monument that names each person who participated in that miracle. Instead, I will simply be dazzled by the One who called, empowered, and set them free to respond.

VITAL SIGNS ⌒

Years ago during a physical exam, I asked a doctor if he had any tips for boosting my energy. I can still hear his answer, "I'll tell you what I do, Paul. On my way to work, I swing by Dunkin' Donuts for a cup of coffee. Around midafternoon, when I start to feel droopy, an ice cold Coca-Cola gives me the energy I need to finish the day." I waited for a punch line, but the man was serious.

Most doctors, though, are vast storehouses of useful information, and this is why I tend to pester them with questions. During a physical exam, doctors want to be sure that our vision, heartbeat, and cholesterol levels are normal. Then there's the mysterious knee tap. Have you ever wondered why doctors do that? I asked. It turns out, if your foot bounces forward at even the slightest touch below the knee, your nervous system is functioning properly. A lack of responsiveness or an exaggerated kick would indicate that something is going awry inside of you. It might indicate leprosy, nerve inflammation, or one of more than a dozen other ailments. Translation? With our bodies, proportionate responsiveness is a sign of good health.

In the realm of our souls, we are no different. Proportionate responsiveness is evidence of *spiritual* vitality. Dreaming God's dreams, being moved by God's passions, seeing our world through his eyes, listening and responding proportionately to the fluctuating circumstances around us are vital signs of a thriving faith. My family can testify that listening doesn't exactly come naturally to me. Recently Josiah said, "Dad, I'm going to ride my bike every day, just like you."

I could hear my ten-year-old son's words, but I was deaf to his heart. "Hey, that's wonderful, Josiah! Riding your bike is a great way to keep yourself fit." The next afternoon Josiah asked me if I would ride *with* him. That sounded fun, but I still had quite a bit of work to do that day. "Maybe early next week." Later that night I suddenly woke up with a start. The room was dark, but in that moment I was able to hear the voice of my son's heart with vivid clarity. Josiah had quietly observed that each afternoon I ride my bicycle up into the hills around our city. These rides give me time to think and much-needed exercise. Josiah, though, was not thinking about fitness. He wanted time with his dad, and he saw bike riding as a possible way to squeeze himself into my schedule. Josiah's heart was quietly calling, "Daddy, I crave more *time* together with you!" I hadn't been listening. Instead, I'd been plodding in step with my own tune, and the trumpets, trombones, and tubas in my head were deafening me to the acoustics in my son's heart.

Responsiveness always flourishes in the context of humility because it requires that we take our focus off of ourselves and instead tune our hearts in to the *other*. Purposefully allowing the *other* to lead in the dance of life is not easy for independent-minded people like me, who tend to blaze our own trenches and bulldoze our highways into the future. I am, after all, a product of civilization. My tribe tends to equate following with "throwing in the towel." Submissiveness is usually juxtaposed with leadership. Leading is seen as a virtue. Consequently, responding implies weakness. This way of thinking suffocates our spiritual vitality.

Responsive people would probably not be heard saying, "I am the master of my circumstances." A statement like this seems hollow in a world where tsunamis, accidents, sickness, earthquakes, dirty diapers, closed-minded bosses, and other well-disguised opportunities wreak havoc on the plans and flow charts we mark out for ourselves. Instead of seeing ourselves as the masters of our universe, God simply calls us to open our eyes and become responsive to the astoundingly fruitful opportunities he sends in our direction moment by moment throughout each day.

The greatest level of responsiveness any person can enjoy is being in step with the voice of the Spirit of God. Last night our family was out for pizza with our friend Ginny. Ginny is a nineteen-year-old photographer who came to live in Indonesia for the summer. In the car Ginny mentioned that she relies on the Spirit of God to tell her when to shoot the next picture. She said, "Inevitably those pictures turn out the best." For some, Ginny's comment might seem bizarre. A decade ago, if I'd heard a photographer say that God tells her when to snap a picture, I would have wondered if a few nuts and bolts were missing upstairs. That was before I began to understand the intimate journey of faith God holds out for each of us. Ginny doesn't compartmentalize God. She doesn't keep him in the distant past or shove the lover of her soul away from the details of her life. Her faith is alive and beating in her heart, and it affects her every response.

Responsiveness has nothing to do with overreacting, flaring up, or lashing out. Responsiveness is not being passive, and it doesn't imply living without dreams and ambitions. Responsiveness is cultivating a symbiotic relationship with change. Having this relationship entails embracing our circumstances rather than shying away from them. Responsive people don't fantasize about being rock stars or waste time imagining what it would be like to have prettier wives or wealthier husbands. Instead, they receive their identities, their physical appearances, their names, their talent sets, and the times and places they live in. All of these are gifts from God. Whereas others tend to get tangled up in changing circumstances, responsive people ride change like surfers ride waves.

PREDICTABLE FLUCTUATION ∽

When we lived in California, some of our friends formed a comedy troupe and invited Cyndi to be a part. They performed in clubs around Hollywood and Los Angeles. After being around that environment for a while, I realized that many such performers spend weeks or even months preparing a ten-minute scripted routine. They stand in front of a mirror and hone their punch lines to perfection. From one venue to another, they repeat the same routines dozens of times.

Wouldn't it be wonderful if you and I could wake up each morning knowing exactly what situations we will encounter and so prepare our lines and actions in advance? Life just isn't this way. The other day I was having breakfast at a café with some friends when my cell phone rang. It was my friend Peter on the line, calling from another city. His wife, Adriana, had just suffered a stroke. Peter was close to tears. He asked me to get over to his house and drive Adriana to the hospital. Instantly, my day changed. Apologizing to my friends, I tossed some money on the table and rushed away. My western omelet was abandoned to the flies. Everything but Adriana had to be put aside — and for good reason.

Our lives are a conversation, a relationship, an interplay, and a nonstop series of actions and reactions in the triangulation between God, us, and the world around us. We all sometimes crave predictability. Yet God calls us to courageously move out into the world and to listen for his voice. He calls us to respond with a delicate touch to the constant fluctuations that we encounter. We are like falcons in flight, sent out with purpose from our Master's hand, navigating blustery wind currents.

Living an unscripted life is an art form. On stage they sometimes call it "improv." A genuine improv artist has the audacity to stand before a crowd of people without a clear vision of what will happen. Because of the unpredictable nature of each moment, the audience can feel the tension in the air. Taking cues and inspiration from other artists and from the onlookers, creativity surges in response to what the improv artist sees and hears.

In music we call it "jazz." Some feel that jazz is the highest form of music because it represents creativity beyond composition. Jazz is creativity in motion. No song is ever repeated in exactly the same way. Jazz relies on musicians listening, trusting, and responding to one another in real time.

In sports we see improvisational fluidity when two teams leave the drudgery of practice and take the field under the stadium lights to engage in a struggle for victory. Excitement accompanies movement, decision, strategic action, reaction, and a counterresponse. The greatest athletes are not always the fastest and the strongest. They are the ones who best synchronize their responses to each unfolding moment.

God is calling us to thrive in the hand-in-glove relationship between his creative initiative and human responsiveness. On the pages ahead, you will be called to respond to God's passions, dreams, and purposes for the world you live in. We'll rummage in the depths of faith to find whatever it takes to set us free to respond to God's voice. We'll awaken and hone our creative response—meaning any action that engages and transforms a broken, meaningless, or chaotic situation for the pleasure of God—to the world around us. When faith is removed from abstract intellectualism and is instead triangulated in the interplay between God's voice and life's fluctuations, we discover what it means to walk in the Spirit. God is leading us to engage in a blend of creative tension, risk taking, trust in others, and the constant honing of our responses to the paralyzing moments and hidden opportunities we find ourselves facing. When these elements merge together, we find ourselves playing at the edge. Moment by moment, we are called to consider our world as it is *right now* and say, "I'll take whatever is thrown in my face, and I'll respond by creating something inspiring, beautiful, and honoring to my Creator."

Our days are filled with hidden opportunities to play on the edge, where God's grace touches the world's face. Edges are scary, but they are where change happens. Let's discover together the art of triangulation—listening to God, responding to his voice, and worshiping him through our creative responses to the world around us.

CHAPTER 2

ENGAGE

SWEPT INTO GOD'S DREAMS

Six weeks after Josiah was released from Children's Hospital, my family was back on our feet and ready once again to leave for Indonesia. How I looked forward to that magical airplane ride! The determination in my eyes was back, and I carried a way-too-confident grin. Waving good-bye to our family and friends in Los Angeles, Cyndi and I picked up Katie and Josiah and excitedly boarded a Boeing 747.

Twenty-six hours later, an airplane crew popped open the door of our plush, air-conditioned jet. I was struck by a wall of suffocating heat. I almost choked on the humidity. My shirt was instantly soaked by my own sweat. Nearly two hours later, after facing a scowling immigration officer and gathering our belongings onto a cart, we made our way through a heavy fog of cigarette smoke, out of the crowded airport, and into our new lives.

As we found our way along the chaotic streets to the community where we were going to make our home, I felt as though an endless sea of humanity was pressing in on me. No wonder, I had just moved my family to one of the most densely populated islands on earth.

Our home was located in a crowded *kampung*. In those days our city had no system to deal with refuse. Rat-infested mountains of stinking garbage lined the streets and alleys. We settled into our house and tried to figure out how to live. It was almost impossible to rest, and I wondered *when* people slept. Just outside our bedroom window, a motorcycle mechanic plied his trade until late into the night. Sometimes even after midnight, the irritating whine of two-stroke motors being revved up to full throttle kept us tossing and turning.

Each morning, what little sleep we had spirited away from the noisy darkness was suddenly shattered by the sound of loudspeakers in five mosques calling our community to prayer at 4:00 a.m. As our neighbors began their daily routines, we were awakening to confusion. Day after day, we were reduced. We felt like terrified, screaming toddlers who had lost sight of their parents. Within a few weeks, we were robbed, used, lied to, and cheated. After killing seventeen rats in our house, I stopped counting. Perhaps even worse, we were awash in a sea of unfamiliar cultural nuances. I desperately missed everything about America.

Nowadays, Cyndi and I can laugh about that rude introduction to our new lives. Now we see so clearly what God was doing. Providentially, God was carrying us through a rapid succession of faith-defining moments. Would our circumstances roll over us like giant waves, crushing our spirits and sending us scurrying back to a more familiar world of ease and predictability? Would the pressures of making our way through these challenges divide us, wreak havoc on our family life, and send our marriage into disarray?

For a while it sure seemed that way.

Initially the path forward appeared impossible. In fact, it *was* impossible. God wanted us to understand that the idea of an American family moving to another part of the world, believing we are going to have any sort of lasting impact there, is just plain ridiculous. He wanted to show *me* that I was steeped in arrogance and that I was in way over my head. Thankfully, God didn't abandon me to my ego. He brought me to my knees to show me who the real World Changer is. Cyndi and I had no choice but to cry out to him for our physical, spiritual, mental, and emotional survival. Now we understand that God's purpose was to show us how his mighty river of strength surges in the blessed void created by human frailty. In his perfect time, God would take our family by the hand, lift us up, and lovingly lead us through the darkness. His Spirit was to rush from within us, stronger, fuller, and richer with each new challenge. God not only began to strengthen our responsiveness to adversity, but he beckoned Cyndi and me to rise into his breathtaking dreams for the world around us.

GOD'S DREAMS ∽

Johannes was a river of quiet wisdom, an ocean of faith. Striding through life with a cheerful grin on his face, Johannes was a board member at the international school where I had been serving for two years as the principal. Once in a while, without calling first, he'd drive to campus in his dented van to have a relaxed talk. Whether my schedule was heavy or light, if he poked his face into my office, it was time to drop everything and pour some coffee.

Johannes knew I was working my dream job. In spite of my shock at the living conditions, the working part was exhilarating. I was a fulfilled thirty-one-year-old having a lot of fun. I had been entrusted with leading an amazing community of kids and teachers. The students came from all over the world, and many of them were on their way to attending world-class universities. They asked great questions and even laughed at some of my jokes. Every day I worked alongside positive, dedicated teachers who cared about developing a state-of-the-art school. In my second year, we purchased a larger property and mapped out our plans for a sprawling, grassy campus overlooking the city. We constructed a towering gymnasium and installed a teakwood basketball floor. Talented teachers were coming from America to join our staff. Everybody was excited about our momentum.

Johannes, however, didn't want to talk about our success. "Paul, this weekend I'm going out to speak in a village church. There's a small Christian school there. Why don't you come along and get to know some of my friends?"

I agreed to tag along. We passed through villages and over dirt roads, bumping past rice paddies, through misty valleys, and across makeshift tire-and-log bridges spanning dizzying canyons. As we gazed far down onto the roaring rapids below, Johannes talked about the broken condition of education in Indonesia. He lamented the 20,000 children in our province who couldn't afford to go to school. Whether they lived in large, sprawling cities or in more remote villages, an overwhelming number of kids were in a no-win situation. They begged on the streets, joined gangs, or labored in shadowy factories. Johannes described what it was like to be a child sharing benches in crowded classrooms with up to fifty children crammed together in front of one teacher.

He described stressed headmasters who whipped children's hands with bamboo canes for being late to school. Johannes explained that people across the islands, whether Christian, Buddhist, Hindu, or Muslim, all shared a common hunger for better education.

As Johannes painted his thoughts, I slowly began to envision, for the first time, the plight of the children all around me — and not just the kids at *my* school. He repeatedly invited me to speak to children and teenagers eager for a glimpse of hope. I walked across the dirt floors of small Christian schools that could not afford a single book or box of chalk. On "bowl of rice" salaries, Christian teachers were planting seeds of hope in the hearts of children.

As I interacted with these men and women, it dawned on me that Indonesia, which had long been stuck in a cycle of generational poverty and hopelessness, already contained the raw materials for a miraculous explosion of transformation. As in many other developing countries, God had already infused Indonesia with all of the natural resources any nation could want. All of the resources she so desperately sought were buried in the hearts, minds, and souls of her own children. I began to realize that Indonesia's future would never be seriously impacted by short-term, band-aid strategies, or even by the blind transference of money from the West. Instead, the best way I could serve this country was to engage in reaching, awakening, and activating the next generation of Indonesian leaders. Visions of Indonesian youngsters rising, thriving, and leading their own nation began to materialize in my brain.

Johannes affirmed that I would be free to travel virtually anywhere if I were engaged with peoples' needs, especially the needs of children. God was using another person to reorient me into something he deeply cared about. In fact, I was a marlin hooked, and God was reeling in my heart.

After that weekend I couldn't get those kids out of my mind. I was becoming intoxicated with the idea that I might be able to respond with a tangible solution to the plight of impoverished children. In the weeks after that trip, I would frequently leave my bed in the darkness and kneel on the living room floor, praying and weeping for those kids. I had no idea how to help them. I had no plan. I didn't know at the time that I would enter a journey of creating learning environments that would take me to unimagined places. The origin of my dream was not an idea or a strategy. It was simply the awakening of my heart. Having looked into peoples' eyes and listened to their voices, my heart welled up in response to a specific human condition that also grieved God's heart.

The book of Nehemiah celebrates the chasing of a dream. I am mesmerized by the way he unwraps God's calling to create a solution in response to a broken condition. He never records one sentence spoken by God, and yet he affirms that it was God who directed his way. He writes that God had *put it in his heart* to build a wall around Jerusalem. Nehemiah provides a glimpse into the inception of his dream. What does it mean to hear God's voice calling? Or, perhaps I should ask, what does it *feel* like to have a dream infused into one's soul?

Nehemiah begins his narrative by showing that his entire journey was in response to something his brother had told him. "Those who survived the exile and are back in the province are in great trouble and disgrace. The wall of Jerusalem is broken down, and its gates have been burned with fire."[1] When Nehemiah caught a glimpse of a broken condition, his immediate response was to sit down and weep. Nehemiah writes that he wept for *days*. During these days of internal affliction, his own heartbeat matched the rhythm of God's heart, resulting in a new dream and the activation of the creative process. We see a similar moment of fusion when the apostle Paul walked into the city of Athens. Luke writes that "he was greatly distressed to see that the city was full of idols."[2] Something beyond Paul stirred a passion within him to respond. Similarly, when we open up our hearts to the world around us, we are positioning ourselves to be moved by the heart of God and swept into his dreams.

ELECTRIFIED

I don't know of any sound as soothing and romantic as cloud water pattering on the wide, green banana leaves just outside our bedroom window early on a Saturday morning. Yet where I live, rain doesn't always portend snuggling and hot chocolate. In fact, it can often generate irritating problems. Here, almost every day for six months of the year, the thundering, battleship gray sky opens up with all of her might and bombards us with her artillery. Houses are often flooded, delicate gurgling brooks rampage, and streets become rivers of mud. Most irritatingly, with virtually every downpour, someone downtown decides to flip some mysterious switch to Off, resulting in widespread blackouts. The electricity suddenly blinks out, followed by a moment of unexpected silence and a loud chorus of groans. The sudden darkness can be all too frustrating in the evenings, especially when one of us has just purchased hotels on Boardwalk and Park Place and is about to sink the rest of the family into bankruptcy.

The loss of electricity usually originates from downtown, but not always. The culprit could possibly be an American guest in our house who brought with her a hair dryer. Our house doesn't get along with those gadgets. One night our lights blinked out, leaving our family in total darkness. The first thing I do when the lights go off is look out the window to see if everyone else has gone dark as well. If our neighbors' lights are still on, then it's just our problem. On this particular night, I saw lights next door, which meant that we had simply blown a fuse. So I said to my son who was six years old at the time, "Stephen, can you please solve the problem?"

His cute little voice answered in the darkness, "I don't know how, Daddy."

I wasn't going to give up that easily. I had a teachable moment in my hands. This was a chance for him to tone his responsiveness in a moment of adversity. "Give it your best try, son. Please respond to the problem."

There was a long silence. His mind was shifting into gear. "Do you want me to go up on the roof, Daddy?"

"Why would you want to go up on the roof?"

"Well, I could get the satellite dish and bring it down here, then we could all have our lights back." Interesting kid. All this time he had reckoned that our light somehow entered the house through the dish on the roof. In this conversation, Stephen had been engaged by a problem. Then, instead of running, panicking, complaining, screaming in agony, blaming someone else, assuming that someone else would deal with it, or worst of all, pretending the problem doesn't exist, he responded to it. The moment that he started thinking of a possible solution, he positioned himself to be a problem solver. His initial strategy was nutty, but that's okay. At least his imagination was humming. He was grappling, searching in his mind, trying to figure out a solution. We found a flashlight and went outside to locate the fuse box. When I let him open the door of the box and press his tiny finger against the red button, he was fascinated by what he had found.

Stephen's interest had been electrified.

Our Father, too, leads us to join with him in an active response to the problems and broken conditions around us—hurting people, sour relationships, situations at work that feel unassailable, fears, and even family secrets that have been off limits for conversation. We must find the courage to reverse the way that we see the world around us. We all face the temptation to run and hide from problems, to drown ourselves in vicarious living, empty entertainment, and useless fantasies. God wants us to run toward the problems and needs around us, seeing them as opportunities to reveal his glory. Faith is always relevant in time and space. The God who surrounds us draws our minds, hearts, and bodies closer to the elements and the hearts around us, not farther away. Those who live by faith sink their teeth into reality and don't let go. God beckons us to notice the colors, textures, and fluctuating circumstances he gives us right now, and he moves us into a proportionate responsiveness.

During my own solitary nights of praying for the children and youth all across these islands, I was grasped, lifted, and carried into a response. There was an immediate twinge of fear, because the problem that ignited my dream was enormous. More than once I reasoned, "How can I possibly do anything with these dinky talents of mine?" I could relate to Moses, who panicked when God called him to launch a movement of freedom for slaves, saying, "I am slow of speech and tongue."[3] Many of my friends who have been drawn into God's dreams have similar stories. Some wondered if they were too old. Others felt unprepared. Most of us don't communicate well in front of audiences. We feel sluggish. We have trouble with blood sugar. Financial resources are scarce. Yet we long to respond in some way, to look within ourselves and say, "Do I have *anything* at all that can possibly help?"

Taking whatever resources, talents, and abilities that have been entrusted to us, no matter how small, God's dreamers step forward. We are startled to find that our tiny seeds of faith begin to grow. Our little becomes exactly the amount that God needs to work his perfect will in our hurting world.

In my free time I could think of little else but creating schools in response to what God had shown me. I lay in bed imagining high-impact learning environments, places where loving and caring Christian teachers would raise up their nation's future leaders. At breakfast I talked excitedly with Cyndi about starting schools that would give impoverished children a chance to chase their dreams. The students would learn to solve problems and develop tenacious character. The graduates would become skilled and trained communicators who, as undaunted leaders, would impact every domain of their society for Christ. These schools would become wellsprings of change and fountains of creative energy that would pour out their graduates to a thirsty nation.

Nothing this powerful had ever grabbed hold of my heart before. These were not simply fleeting ideas dancing in my head. Nor were they a *vision* of the future, in the sense that God was showing me a focused picture of where I was going. They felt more like the deep, resonant notes of a bass guitar pounding in my heart.

BASS LINES ∽

I was in the audience when U2 came to Anaheim Stadium on their 1992 Zoo TV tour. U2 is one of the rare acts that sounds even better on stage than in a recording studio, and for this reason I've been willing to camp outside to get tickets. U2 fans admire how the band has somehow not forgotten their roots while simultaneously exploring new territory. Yet something else about this band has always intrigued me. Behind the glitter of thirty-two video monitors, under the cars hanging in open space above the stage, beyond the entrancing melodies of Edge's guitar, and even beneath Bono's charismatic persona, stands the band's best-kept secret: Adam Clayton, the bass player.

A band can be a collection of diverse musicians from various musical genres, each playing a different instrument. Yet they can create beautiful music together only if they are each synchronizing themselves with the bass guitar, which is usually playing a repeated chord progression. Most people in the audience rarely look at the bass player. Our attention is usually caught up in the bright lights and drama at the front of the stage. Yet the secret to listening to any great rock song is tuning in to the one guy who keeps playing the same notes. For me, a bass line is like the heart beat of a song. Along with the percussions, the bass guitarist establishes the depth and the power of the song. Most important, the bass line establishes the foundation upon which the other musicians can improvise. If an entire band is following a singer, their music will rapidly unravel. But if they are tuned in to the bass, their music has a chance to come through beautifully.

Like a great rock 'n' roll band, we are never called to unite around the charisma of any one leader. Instead, God calls us to sync our hearts with the depth and power of his own passions, his bass lines. God is unconcerned with the bloated ego of any mere mortal. He has something much greater in mind. He invites us to be a part of a global network of people who are surging forward together, different yet sharing his dreams that pulse within us.

Granted, dreamers might *feel* alone as they take their initial steps of faith. Yet they find that God rarely infuses a dream into just one person's heart. Eventually, those who have the courage to strike out alone are delighted to find, as Elijah did in his most desperate moments of solitude, that God is simultaneously at work through seven thousand others.[4] From a distance we might associate a movement of the Spirit, the explosion of an organization, the growth of a church, or a paradigm shift with one particular leader. To be sure, many leaders have an important role as visionaries and communicators. Yet, as we come closer, we will always discover a band of people who have stepped out by faith in response to the dreams the Spirit has planted in their hearts. A dream may be initially sparked in one soul, yet God commands battalions rather than Rambo-like characters to accomplish his purposes. Our individual egos burst into flames as our God-given dreams sweep into the hearts of others.

Bruce Ellis Benson wrote this intriguing insight, "To improvise in jazz ... is to respond to a call, to join in something that is always already in progress."[5] As I began to share my new passion with others, I quickly found God weaving a group of artists together to respond to his call; we were drawn together to share in the fellowship of God's creative process. Within months a community of people had stepped forward to unite ourselves in efforts to launch the flagship school. I found myself surrounded and even carried along by others who were much smarter and more capable than I. God's bass line pounded in our hearts as we struggled to forge a new model of transformational Christian education that would shape Indonesia's future leaders. Experienced teachers dedicated themselves to train others. Board members were commissioned. Others volunteered time, talent, and money. Various donors sacrificed financially, giving joyfully for the initial costs of equipment purchases. Others decided to help with scholarships. Parents signed up their children for this new venture. I had never seen such an eclectic group of people united around one passion.

STORM CLOUDS ༒

Almost immediately this little movement of dreamers faced complications. We were warned that the government of the largest Islamic nation on earth would never tolerate the launching of openly Christian schools, especially by people whose stated purpose is to impact the world for Christ. Every attempt to secure permission to open a Christian school from Islamic authorities would require another miracle. Initially, we were faced with a conundrum. Would we be attacked? Would our schools get burned down? Should we somehow try to go underground? Should we be secretive about this endeavor?

Each time I wrestled with these fears, Jesus' words thumped in my heart, "A city on a hill cannot be hidden. Neither do people light a lamp and put it under a bowl. Instead they put it on its stand, and it gives light to everyone in the house. In the same way, let your light shine before men."[6] We had no other choice, really. We realized that one day lived in the light is better than many years of slinking around in the shadows. God wanted our schools to be a highly visible presence in this nation. He wanted us to shine his light all around, even to the authorities. He was calling us to serve humanity, to offer to train Muslim teachers, and to set the pace for all education, not just Christian education. God wanted the world around us to see and give him glory because of what was happening.

Granted, on any given day, our circumstances could swiftly change. I suppose the entire operation could be smashed to pieces tomorrow. My friends and I might even find ourselves expelled, assaulted, or locked up. That's in God's hands. So far, at least, he has given us favor with the authorities and has opened one door after another.

Chasing God's dreams always entails a certain risk. Jesus said that whatever he tells us in the dark should be proclaimed in the light. Whatever he whispers in our ears should be shouted from the rooftops.[7] His words remind us to look beyond this short breath of life in this world. His voice bears forward into eternity. "Do not be afraid of those who kill the body but cannot kill the soul."[8] Is God's voice calling you to rise up into his dreams? Does his bass line seem to involve mystery and danger? As you step forward, the temptation to retreat into the safe havens of the past will always be there. Be assured that he will providentially lead you into seemingly blind alleys. In these impossible moments, you will look ahead to see only dangerous turns, dead ends, and ominous obstacles. Behind you will be the same road you traveled yesterday, and that pattern of existence will feel inviting. You'll want to put life into reverse and get back to familiar streets. In these moments of decision, many dreams get stored away in the musty, cobwebbed basements of our souls.

Yet such alleys are where miracles happen. Crises are the launching pads from which God blasts us into a journey of faith. When all appears to be lost, we are left with no choice but to fall to our knees and cry out to God. We then discover that moments of impossibility are precisely where God has always wanted us. In these moments our lives become the playground of his creativity.

The ultimate honor and glory are always God's. In Indonesia we've discovered that God's dreams result in organic movements that grow, thrive, and take on a life of their own. Since those initial days of creating our first school, others have emerged, hundreds of teachers have been trained, and at this point approximately 2,900 children are being impacted in these programs each day. Learning environments of various textures have been established, spawning new movements in early-childhood education, community education centers for kids who can't afford to go to school, and youth centers designed to offer hope to teenagers on the streets. Graduates are moving toward positions of influence as entrepreneurs, physicians, nurses, filmmakers, writers, and professional athletes.

These days, my friends and I can walk across campuses that once existed solely in God's imagination. We now see with our eyes what God once planted in our hearts. We hear the voices of hundreds of children who are learning, creating, singing, praying, and growing. Each morning we meet together to celebrate our Creator, and even now the Spirit of Christ is planting new dreams and visions within us.

DUST THEORY ⁓

I was eleven years old when I first heard the song "Dust in the Wind" by Kansas drifting fuzzily through my wood-paneled clock radio. Little did I know that I was listening to the cardinal philosophy of the times: "All my dreams pass before my eyes, a curiosity. Dust in the wind, all they are is dust in the wind."

There's nothing new about the idea that we have no reason to hang on and that our dreams are nothing more than dust in the wind. Whether it was Noah cutting down trees to build an ark, William Wilberforce pleading in the British House of Commons to abolish slavery, or William Carey opening Christian schools for girls in India, individuals who step outside their safety zones and move to the edge to chase God's dreams have always been ridiculed.

In our own lifetime, disengagement from God's dreams has been epidemic. Are your dreams feeling a bit subdued these days? We've been surrounded, pummeled, and anesthetized by dust theory. Progress, eliminating extreme poverty, and reaching out to the world with the radical story of Jesus' life, death, and resurrection are supposedly flavors of the past. Society is telling us to hunker down, order a latte, and live for ourselves.

Perhaps this widespread aloofness has something to do with being born during the Vietnam War and raised under the threatening skies of the Cold War. My friends and I grew up convinced that on any given day some nameless janitor mopping the floor of an office in Moscow might just be tempted to press a red button and end the world. In junior high we'd huddle around lunch tables in the school cafeteria, sipping from our little chocolate-milk cartons, envisioning ourselves surviving like the Road Warrior in the fallout of a dystopian world. We'd talk about skin melting off of skeletons and wonder when the entire planet would end in annihilation.

Even as we grew older, we tended to roll our eyes at foolish, breathless dreamers who spoke of changing the world. We loved to complain about the emptiness of life. It became trendy to believe that we're just a bunch of cogs in the machinery of some great, cosmic conspiracy. Dust theory became funny. Television relentlessly celebrated the idea that we have no authority to shape our destiny, and that visionary dreamers are out of style. *Seinfeld* and *Friends* celebrated nothingness as they shrank our entire universe into meaningless upper-Manhattan chitchat. Goofy personalities replaced virtuous heroes, and petty annoyances replaced the reality of evil. Meanwhile, our own children sat in the other room watching *Bill and Ted's Excellent Adventure*. The suspenseful plot thickens as two of our era's most distinguished philosophers travel through time to ancient Greece, where they encounter Socrates.

"How's it going? I'm Bill, and this is Ted. We're from the future!"

"Now what?" Ted whispers to Bill.

Bill stammers, "I dunno ... philosophize with him!"

Ted clears his throat and says, "All we are is dust in the wind, dude!"

Socrates stares at them with a confused expression. Bill dramatically scoops up a handful of dust from a basin and lets it drift through his fingers. "Dust ... dude!"

That Kansas song still carries a haunting melody. Yet the aftermath of dust theory isn't quite so humorous. This way of thinking drifted beyond our film studios and philosophy classrooms, through the streets of our cities and settled into the sanctuaries of many of our churches.

AWAKENINGS ∽

When the dust settles into religious environments, it can be toxic. When I was a college student, I began attending a small church located just around the corner from my house. Each Sunday, I enjoyed the pastor's animated Bible teaching. One of my warmest memories is of the deacon who sat in a chair just behind the pastor. The deacon usually slept through most of the messages, only now and then stirring from his slumber to crack open his eyes and shout a hearty Amen! The timing of these outbursts rarely coincided with a meaningful point, and it was obvious to everyone in the church that the deacon had not a clue about what he was agreeing to.

One Sunday the pastor was emphasizing that all people are sinners. He said, "Now, *even I* commit sins every single day." At that moment, the deacon stirred from his sleep and shouted a vigorous Amen! We all erupted with laughter and wild applause, including the pastor. In spite of the church's idiosyncrasies, I found comfort in the repeated assertions that the fellowship was committed to solid Bible teaching.

In those days, my roommates and I started a Bible club in our home for children in our neighborhood. On Tuesday afternoons, they piled into our living room. Eventually, the place was so crowded that children were sitting on both our front porch and back porch trying to listen. One morning I paid a visit to our pastor, to ask him if the Bible club could have access to the church's basement. Surely he would host a community outreach in the church, which sat as empty as a haunted house through most of the week.

Even now, I can still see the man sitting in his office chair explaining to me that the children would probably break the windows of the church and trample the new carpet. Besides, if his insurance company found out, the monthly payments would likely go through the roof. I walked home that day feeling that Christianity was starving, emaciated by a famine of dreams. Having closed ourselves off from God's passion to pour his love through us into the world around us, I felt that we had been rendered blind to the challenges and opportunities that God so freely placed into our paths. It seemed that the dust lay thick in my church, despite the biblical sermons.

Have you ever found yourself wondering what happened to the dynamic movement of the Spirit of the living God that was so long ago unleashed into human history with an exultant declaration of visions and dreams? Do you ever live with the impression that much of Christianity has been sidelined, like a crowd of survivors sitting in the mud of a refugee camp, helpless and terrified to rise up? You are not alone. Many have been plagued, even tormented, by the same gnawing questions.

There is good news.

Across the globe the dispiriting idea that our dreams are nothing more than dust in the wind is being rendered laughable. The Spirit is blowing across the nations like a hurricane of hope. The signs are everywhere, and they have an unprecedented feel. What we are witnessing is not a revival in the classic sense. In fact, we are being forced to reach for new ways to describe it. Unlike revivals of the past, the impact is not centered on how Christians behave inside our churches. Instead, it has far more to do with how the world around us is being confronted, startled, and awakened by the Spirit's creative movement.

An occupational therapist named Laurie came to live in Indonesia for six months. Laurie was amazed at the scarcity of services for Indonesian children with special needs. While she was here, a boy named Totok was in a horrific motorcycle accident. His skull hit the pavement and cracked open. Totok was rushed to the hospital but was refused treatment unless his relatives showed proof they could pay the bill. Totok spent the better part of a day in the hospital waiting room with the talons of death squeezing the life out of him. Finally, the family came up with some money, and Totok survived surgery. He came home with what appeared to be severe brain damage. In the weeks following his surgery, he could not utter a sentence nor get up from his bed and walk.

Laurie, though, was bent on hope, and she was determined to help. Day after day, she provided intensive therapy. Within weeks, we began to see rapid improvement. Totok is now the striker on our school's varsity soccer team. I recently watched him score four goals in one game. He is also a top student, and has one of the humblest and purest hearts I know. Totok dreams of someday becoming a pastor. One day during the months Laurie was giving therapy to Totok, she asked me to have a look at some lines she had written:

> Walk along a crowded street,
> And thriving souls you would meet,
> Each with visions, dreams and plans,
> For the Spirit flows through man.
>> And in his image God creates
> Dreamers who would hope and wait
> To see their heart's desire unfold,
> And would they shout for joy if told?
>> The dreams resounding in our hearts
> He knew before all time would start.

In fact, he placed them in his sons
And laughed with joy at what he'd done!
      Waves of mercy, winds of grace,
Capacity to dream he placed
On children who won't stay the same;
The Spirit always changes things.
      Express his Passions! Lift your hands!
Advance his Kingdom in this land.
Stay the evil one's intent,
And we will soar as we were meant.

The prophet Isaiah wrote of a man who denies himself food in order to break the bands of wickedness, to undo the heavy burdens, to let the oppressed go free and break every yoke, to provide food for the hungry, and to clothe the naked. He wrote that this man's light will break forth like the dawn and that the glory of God would be his rear guard, and that his night would become like the noon day.[9] With souls on fire, men and women who dream God's dreams are advancing against the forces of evil that wage war against God and his creation.

Recently I was in Kolkata, India, with my friends Subir and Eunok. In the early 1990s, this couple began to serve families from the untouchable caste. As we made our way along the streets of the city (once known as Calcutta), Subir explained that it is commonly believed untouchables don't have souls. Uncounted thousands of these people live in shantytowns and sleep under the open sky. Initially, Subir and Eunok had very few resources but did whatever possible to respond to the needs of homeless families and unwanted children. They provided food for the hungry and launched open-air evangelism programs for children. Over the years, God has given them increased momentum. Now they have eight Christian schools and two children's homes. About 3,000 children in the vicinity of Kolkata are being helped by these programs. Sixty house churches have sprung up, and four larger churches have been planted in the communities around the eight schools.

Subir and Eunok invited me to visit their shelter for discarded infants. I picked up a beautiful baby girl and was holding her in my arms when I noticed that she had dozens of tiny scars all over her body. Eunok explained that from the time the girl was a newborn, her father had made a habit of extinguishing his cigarettes on her skin. I could see God's passionate love for that baby girl burning in Eunok's and Subir's eyes. Their hearts are blazing with dreams to seek and save children like this.

The idea of "dreams" has tended to carry a fuzzy meaning. A sixteen-year-old fantasizes that she will be Miss South Dakota. Her little sister longs to bring home that little poodle from the pet store. Her older brother imagines himself surfing the Pipeline in Hawaii. Her mom longs to visit Italy, while her father closes his eyes and thinks about what it would feel like to finally retire.

Those are old-school dreams.

Not to belittle them. Cyndi and I dream of having enough yard space so we can plant a garden of our own. We could raise our own tomatoes, corn, and carrots. We'd also cultivate raspberries and strawberries if they could handle the climate. Ah, that would be so fun. But in comparison with the bass line pounding in our hearts, that dream is really just a fantasy. Today's dreams have a spirited feel. So many people are tuning into God's heartbeat for the world. Longing to live with greater purpose and driven by their passion to serve, they would think nothing of resettling in the most impoverished communities on earth. These dreams are God's way of sweeping us into his plans and purposes. They are what our souls have always longed for, the high-voltage dreams that originate in God's own heart. Their inception is the unblinking awareness that something is in conflict with God's original intention for his creation. A marriage is dying, perhaps, or a child is lost. A community is being taken over by drug lords. A village has no access to clean water. A tsunami has wiped out half of a city. A crippling epidemic is sweeping through a continent, or perhaps Grandpa can't read.

Something somewhere is in a fallen state, waiting "in eager expectation for the sons of God to be revealed."[10] Acute awareness of the problem creates angst in the soul. Most of us would rather not live with this feeling. Mistakenly believing that this *angst* is the problem, rather than a portal into God's miracles, many turn away or drown it out by various means. A life of creativity is traded in for surfing the Internet, vicarious living, drowning in television, or playing video games. All the while these individuals remain blissfully unaware that they have just disqualified themselves from chasing God's dreams, which is one of the most joyful and exhilarating experiences in all of life.

Others find the courage to respond to the angst. For them, the discomfort only increases as they lie awake at night, imagining how the world would be experienced if somehow the broken and fallen condition were to be redeemed. They position their souls to be ignited with dreams, which are conceived in the moment that the Spirit of God moves to infuse into them a passion to respond. Here we must not confuse dreams with ideas. Most ideas melt away very quickly. Yet a dream is much more profound. It is like an idea that grips our souls and won't let go.

It has the power to keep a person awake night after night. It may arrive in the form of a song, a poem, an architectural innovation, or a breakthrough insight into an old problem. However it comes, we are stirred by its boldness and originality.

Recently, a college student named Christin came to Indonesia for a visit. Christin plays for a large university on a tennis scholarship. In high school she was the second-ranked player in her state. As a top student, she has the ability to do virtually anything she wants with her future. Her heart has been captured by a dream to serve impoverished children. Christin spent one summer in Cairo, Egypt, where she was involved serving homeless and orphaned kids who live in a trash dump. She's already been to South America and to China.

Christin is in the early stages of absorbing God's dreams into her heart, and I can't wait to see where those dreams carry her. She is not alone. We have witnessed wave after wave of people coming to developing countries to lay down their lives for God's purposes. This movement is not limited to the western hemisphere. Here in Indonesia, men and women are awakening to the possibilities before them. Many of our own Indonesian teachers in our schools are dreaming of someday opening Christian schools in Africa. Something very special is going on. Whether God's dreams carry you across the world or across the hallway in your apartment building, know that you are joining others who are also living their faith at the edge.

DREAMING AHEAD ∞

The apostle Paul dreamed of seeing the gospel of Jesus bring freedom to the city of Rome. He purposefully sacrificed his own freedom to go there in chains and be executed. While sitting in a dungeon, contemplating what some people might have perceived as a pitiful, wasted ending to an amazing life, could he have imagined the thousands of souls in that very city who, in the next generation, would surrender their lives for Christ as they were fed to Nero's lions and burned to death on his torches?

History is forged by those who dream and step forward by faith to see their dreams become a living reality. Quoting words from Isaiah and repeated in the gospel of Luke, Martin Luther King Jr. proclaimed, "I have a dream that one day, every valley shall be exalted, every hill and mountain shall be made low, the rough places will be made straight, and the glory of the Lord shall be revealed and all flesh shall see it together." Men like John Adams and Nelson Mandela have taken action for human freedom. People like Viv Grigg and Mother Teresa have stepped out by faith on behalf of the poor. Harriet Beecher Stowe, Harriet Tubman, and Abraham Lincoln dreamed on behalf of slaves then dedicated themselves to seeing their dreams fulfilled. George Mueller's heart was infused with a dream for orphaned children, and he ended up providing a home and education for 23,000 of them. Many have suffered deeply while chasing their dreams. John Bunyan was imprisoned. William Tyndale was strangled and burned at the stake. Jim Elliot and his friends were speared to death.

Jesus was nailed to a cross to see his dream fulfilled.

Some of the greatest dreamers are still waiting to be born. God's dreams are beginning to rain down on the body of Christ, setting us free to become a surging movement of the love in his heart. Has God begun to whisper a dream into your soul? Don't be intimidated by the cynical dust theory that our society so cherishes—not everything is meaningless. You only get to live in this world once. Each moment is a treasured gift from God. Every night when you fall asleep, another day has drifted away, disappearing down the ever-flowing river of time into your memories. Yesterday can never be retrieved. Tomorrow morning, rise up with a radical faith that expects the impossible. Offer your heart to God's passions and invite him to activate his dreams in you. Talk about them over your next cup of coffee. Whisper them to your children as you kiss them good night. May the Spirit of Christ advance through your life and make his eternal imprint in the world around you.

CHAPTER 3

❧

ABSORB

TOUCHED BY GOD'S BREATH

In 1939 a small airplane crashed into the jungle somewhere in Africa. Everyone on board perished in the tragic accident except a baby boy. The infant was discovered by a chimpanzee and carried to the tree house of a man named Tarzan and his wife, Jane. Tarzan and Jane had no children of their own, so they decided to adopt the infant. The animal kingdom waited in eager anticipation for the announcement of the child's name. Tarzan thumped his chest, filled the jungle with a robust scream, and held his new son aloft. "His name shall be called ... Boy!"

Boy? Granted, Tarzan had a tight schedule, running the jungle and all. To make matters worse, he lived in a black and white existence, but couldn't the man drum up something a bit more imaginative? I wonder if Jane agreed to this name. I've come across some outlandish names that really grabbed my attention. I know a guy whose given name means *Third* in his mother tongue. You guessed it: He was a third-born child. A friend of mine had a student named Lies in his English course. At least these names convey a fair amount of meaning. But *Boy!* This one beats all. Getting paged at Chucky Cheese's is bound to stir up confusion: "Would Boy please come to the cash register?" What happens when Boy grows up? Will he feel insulted when his boss says, "Hey, Boy, when are you going to finish that report?"

In the English language, the word *God* comes across a bit like *Boy*—somewhat vague and hinting at disengaged parents. This word originates in the Germanic *Gott.* Who is this Gott? Where is he or she? Is it similar to Mother Nature? Is it sort of like the Force in *Star Wars*? How can we become responsive to God's dreams and live with a triangulated faith if we don't know much more about him than Aristotle knew about "actuality"? I suppose there's only one way to find out. We must open his story and let this Gott explain himself.

SO FAR, SO CLOSE ∞

The opening lines of any story are pivotal. They introduce us to the author's voice. They set the context. They introduce characters, themes, and conflicts to come. Whether we read "Call me Ishmael" or "In a hole in the ground there lived a hobbit," from those first words we are joining the artist's journey.

In ancient Hebrew writings, passages originally had no chapters, titles, punctuation, or even page numbers, so the initial line also functioned as the title. As Moses hovered over his parchments and began to write the opening paragraph of the Torah, one imagines him being careful to capture the right tone. Not only was this the tale of our universe, it was our inaugural glimpse of God: "In the beginning God created the heavens and the earth.

Now the earth was formless and empty, darkness was over the surface of the deep, and the Spirit of God was hovering over the waters. And God said, 'Let there be light,' and there was light."[1]

You may have read these lines many times before. Even so, try reading them again as if for the first time. They carry us through a sequence of pivotal discoveries. They send us forward, providing context for the rest of his epic story. Straightaway, Moses refers to God with a name, almost as if he were writing something like this, "On the first day of school, Kevin ...." Elohim is a name that signifies God's strength and power. The starting point for everything is this: Elohim existed before anything else. This means that at some point in time Elohim was surrounded by absolute nothingness. Consequently, we learn that Elohim is not a philosophical phantom engaged in endless self-contemplation. Instead, Elohim wades into the primordial void with a startling act of creativity.

God created the heavens. The Hebrew word for "heavens," *shamayim*, refers to the lofty realm of the stars and includes the vast, complex, immeasurable, and mysterious dimensions of reality beyond our finite grasp. We now understand that it includes the sun, the moon, other planets, galaxies, asteroids, black holes, antimatter, angelic beings, and even the transcendent laws by which God sustains his universe. For one sublime moment, the Creator comes across as unimaginably ... far away.

For ages upon ages, our ancestors have been shivering and huddling around their smoky campfires, trying to stay warm while lifting up their eyes, wondering at the light of the heavens. Generation after generation, we have gazed at the night sky and felt so insignificant. As we have grown to understand more about the universe, our wonder has only increased. Scientists are now convinced there are more stars in our universe than there are grains of sand on our entire planet. As we attempt to fathom the idea that there is a being who created a universe that massive, our imaginations are stretched like rubber bands almost beyond capacity. *Gott made all that?* We feel whittled down like forgotten soldiers buried at the bottom of a child's toy box. When faced with the grandeur of God's creative power, we can only fall prostrate on our faces and cry out in the darkness.

Our voices drift into the night wind.

Mornings all across Indonesia begin with the call to prayer from thousands of mosques ringing out over cities and villages. Men and women rise from their beds, slip on their sandals, and walk through a maze of dark alleys to their houses of worship. They line up shoulder to shoulder and drop to their knees in prayer, lowering their faces to the ground. Crying out as Muslims have done for 1,400 years, they pray the mantra, "God is great." Many Muslims affirm, "Yes! God is the Creator of the universe!" For them, the understanding that God is the Creator only magnifies his remoteness and extends his distance. The Creator remains far away and hidden beyond the cosmos. He is silent and has no personality. He is eternally unknowable.

My family and I recently enjoyed a Saturday afternoon in the house of a highly respected imam, a teacher of the Koran, named Setiawan. Setiawan is sixty years old and is dying of cancer. His daughter invited Cyndi and our three children to go outside and walk to a stream that flows over their land. I stayed behind with Setiawan. As we chatted, our conversation soon found its way into the matters of his heart. I shared that God intimately cares about his condition. I asked him if he would allow me to pray for him, and he responded with an eager "Yes!" Setiawan's eyes conveyed a hunger for something he has never found in his regimen: the chance to speak *with* God, to listen for his voice, to be able to approach him with the most personal longings of his heart.

Like Setiawan, many of our Muslim friends are enraptured each time I affirm that the Almighty Creator of the universe also created in response to a woman named Hannah's agonized prayer for a child of her own. In the Bible the God who created the heavens also causes a bed of wildflowers to flourish on the side of a breezy hill. God holds a billion-sun galaxy in his right hand while wrestling with a man named Jacob under the stars.[2] God reveals that he is surprisingly nuanced. Story by story, the One who said, "Let us make man in our image, in our likeness,"[3] beckons us into his depth. Reading through the Bible is a bit like finding out that a Herculean offensive tackle for the Pittsburgh Steelers writes poetry and bakes rhubarb pie. Just like any individual person, God has personality traits. He relates to others through his heart. He loves; he feels sadness, anger, jealousy, and, despite our well-planned, perfectly logical predictions of what he *should* be, he even feels regret.[4] God experiences the full possibilities of passion and creates us to know his passionate heart. God cries out in celebration. He listens and he talks. We are intrigued by statements such as "God said to the woman," "The LORD said to Cain," "God said to Noah," "God said to Abraham," and "God said to Jacob."[5] God sits down with Abraham in his tent, and he chats with Moses as you and I would speak to our closest friends. He whispers to a child named Samuel in his room. He spends time with a boy named David in the shade of a tree and breathes music through his harp.

As Elohim reveals his many other names, he delicately invades our understanding. For those who care to know him, Elohim becomes El Echad, the One. He is El Hanne'eman, the Faithful One. He is El Emet, the Truth; El Shaddai, the All Sufficient; El Gibbor, the Champion and Warrior. He is El Roi, the God who sees *me*; El Chaiyai, the God of *my* life; El Sali, the God of *my* strength; El Rachum, the God of compassion. By the time we reach Isaiah, Elohim is no longer far away. He is Immanuel, God *with* us. From beginning to end, God becomes less distant and more alive. In the matrix of human faith, God reveals himself in the mundane, moving from mystery to increased clarity. God not only approaches in proximity. He approaches in time, advancing from the distant past into this very moment. The God who spoke to Noah, Abraham, and Moses becomes my God *now*.

Throughout his story, Elohim reveals a stunning and invigorating motif. He is a thriving Artist, present in real time, pervasively engaged, and continuously interacting with his creation. The psalmist wrote, "When you send your Spirit, they are created, and you renew the face of the earth."[6] All through the Scriptures, God reveals himself as a craftsman, a carpenter, a composer, a designer, a gardener, a potter, and an author. These creative terms don't refer only to his activities during the original six days of creation, but to his ongoing work in history. Jesus said, "My Father is always at his work to this very day."[7] God *is* the Creator—"the same yesterday and today and forever."[8] The Potter's hands are still covered with clay. The touch of the Potter's hands is sometimes painful, but the finished vessel is a beautiful work of art.

Consider God's creative response to a stretch of desolate wasteland. He shouts exultantly through Isaiah,

I will make rivers flow on barren heights,
   and springs within the valleys.
I will turn the desert into pools of water,
   and the parched ground into springs.
I will put in the desert
   the cedar and the acacia, the myrtle and the olive.
I will set pines in the wasteland,
   the fir and the cypress together,
so that people may see and know,
   may consider and understand,
that the hand of the Lord has done this,
   that the Holy One of Israel has created it.[9]

As I look back over my life, I realize how often the Holy One of Israel has created pools of water and flowing rivers in places where I've seen only parched ground.

GARDENS IN THE DESERT ∽

Anthony was fourteen years old when he and three other Crip gang members took his older brother's car and went looking for trouble. After a few hours of driving around the dimly lit streets of Compton, California, they entered the territory of a rival gang. Anthony and his friends each had .22 caliber handguns tucked into their baggy pants. A veteran of violence, Anthony had already mastered the art of destruction. He had a reputation as a fearless gang leader who could laugh while shooting at an enemy or robbing a convenience store. Allegedly, two of his victims were classmates from elementary school. Other gang members, many of whom were much older, were magnetized by his leadership.

On this night, though, Anthony was not in the mood to kill from the shadows. He would later tell me that he was getting anxious for something more exciting, a more adrenaline-laced method of destruction. In the backseat of the car were a rope and a black garbage bag. Anthony slowly drove past a house where dozens of enemy gang members were drinking and partying. A heavy beat thumped the windows of the dimly lit house. Shadowy figures were standing around in the front yard with bottles of liquor in their hands. He and his friends turned the corner, drove to the darkest place on the block, and turned off the motor. After less than an hour, a young man left the party and started home. His path took him directly past Anthony's car. Anthony and his friends threw open their doors and chased the boy down. They pummeled him with their fists until he was unconscious, dumped him into their trunk, and casually drove home.

Anthony's gang lived in a sprawling, gated housing development on the south side of Compton. When they arrived home in the early hours of the morning, they opened the trunk, tied their victim's hands behind his back, pulled the garbage bag over his head and shoulders, and left him suffocating in the trunk where he screamed, kicked, and writhed in panic until late the next afternoon.

By then a crowd had gathered in front of Anthony's apartment, many of whom were holding baseball bats. Children hung around to see what would happen, as well as men and women returning home from work. They thought they had seen it all, but *never* had they witnessed something quite like this. Anthony's gang had captured a hated enemy and brought him into their own territory, and now they were ready to kill. They pulled the boy out of the trunk and let him run free. His calls for help were muffled by the trash bag as the boy stumbled and fell over the curb. Struggling to his feet, he ran wildly. Some of the onlookers taunted and laughed with glee as the boy blindly slammed into parked cars and tumbled over garbage cans. Anthony watched from his front porch as the crowd eventually tired of the game and beat the boy to death.

A little more than two years later, Anthony walked into my life. Sixteen years old, he had just been released from a detention center for his role in the kidnapping that became a murder. Before he would be allowed to enroll at the local high school, he would need to spend some time with me.

Before moving to Indonesia, I worked for seven years in urban Los Angeles, where I had been commissioned to open a charter school in a Baptist church. My job was to do anything possible to turn around the lives of at-risk teenagers like Anthony. Each day we came alongside youngsters convicted of violent crimes and released from Youth Authority to probation. Because of the high mortality rate of youth in that area, those years were the most arduous of my life. Standing at the graves of students I had grown to love like my own younger brothers, I listened to the wailing screams of grieving mothers, grandmothers, and friends. I was startled by the depth of anguish and hopelessness connected with the urban violence that much of our society has deemed commonplace. In spite of the drive-by shootings and brushes with danger, the funerals and numerous setbacks, I wouldn't trade my years in Compton for anything. Walking the streets of our cities are some of the most inspiring people I've ever known.

In those years God taught me lessons that I will carry with me for the rest of my life. God wanted me to plumb the depth of his immense love for even the most resistant, bitter, and violent youth. He wanted me to learn to listen for his voice and to cry out to him to guide me through every confusing moment. Time after time, he reassured me that when I surrender to his ways rather than insist on my own, I will see his miraculous power in action. The paramount lesson God showed me was that if I desire for him to breathe his life through me, I must learn to trust in the *creative* work of his Spirit.

LET THERE BE LIGHT ∽

There is nothing quite like witnessing a masterful artist create. Have you ever watched an artist like Carlos Santana play a guitar solo, every part of his body, mind, and spirit joined with his instrument to produce a work of musical art? In one of his most riveting discussions capturing the interplay between God and his image bearers, the apostle Paul refers to himself as one of God's "fellow workers."[10] During my years in Compton, I, too, was like an apprentice, studying to be a builder. Each day I witnessed God's creative handiwork; each day I had front-row tickets to the greatest show on earth. The One who spoke the universe into existence performed one miracle after another before my eyes, transforming those whom society had long ago written off.

Most youngsters needed a few weeks with me before they started to thaw out from their perpetual state of inner terror, but not Anthony. He immediately gave the appearance of being in complete control of his own little universe. It was a challenge to keep up with him. Every Sunday morning and Wednesday afternoon I drove from my house in East Los Angeles to Compton to fill the seats of my Toyota 4Runner with gang members and bring them to our church youth group. Anthony loved coming to church. He had never experienced much of anything outside of his gang, and he was immediately intrigued by the love, freedom, and laughter that flowed like a river of life amongst the other kids at church.

That summer Cyndi and I took a group of kids camping at our favorite beach in Mexico, a breathtaking stretch of white sand sloping into the Pacific Ocean two hours south of Tijuana. It was a short drive into Ensenada, where we could bargain for fresh prawns and fish in the harbor market before returning to the beach to drop them into a frying pan sizzling with butter and garlic over an open fire. With Anthony in the passenger seat and a pile of kids sleeping in the back, we drove toward San Diego beneath the moon. Through the night, with the tires on my truck providing a peaceful hum, the Spirit of God began to move his paintbrushes across Anthony's soul.

Anthony pelted me with questions about faith. I asked him to grab my Bible, which was tucked between our seats. He snapped on his lamp so that he could read as I led him from verse to verse. Anthony talked about his internal chaos, describing his urgency to escape from a nightmare of pervasive darkness. Much like his victim just two years before, he felt like he was suffocating internally, without hope, as if his heart were gasping for air. Weak and frail, Anthony was a torn and stranded child caught in the tumbling, swirling rapids between hell and hope. The desperation in his voice revealed the condition of his soul. In response to question after question, I led him from one Scripture to another. Through the night his questions piled up as he struggled to make his way into life, love, purpose, and freedom.

A ray of light was just peeking over the desert hills behind us as we descended from the paved highway onto the sands of our beach. As Anthony saw that our drive was ending, there was a sudden urgency in his voice. He asked me what he should do next. Moments later we were kneeling in the sand together. With tears streaming down his face, Anthony surrendered his soul to his Savior. Just hours later, as a crowd of excited witnesses looked on from the sandy shore and from the heavens, Anthony was baptized in the surging, swirling water of the Pacific Ocean. The wind was not only blowing on his face, but rushing through his soul. The Creator had sent forth his Spirit to make a new creation. Our Creator God had begun a new masterpiece of life.

THE ARTIST ⟩⟩

When trying to grasp who God is, many of us have conjured up something inanimate, something we can easily manipulate, lock inside of a building, plop down in the corner, or push far away, even beyond our consciousness. We imagine the dark cloud on Mount Sinai—then we associate God with this cloud, rather than with the glorious Artist who is making himself visible and audible everywhere around us right now. Some of our society's ideas about God more closely resemble Muhammad's or Aristotle's versions of the Unknowable God rather than the Creator who gave dreams to a younger brother named Joseph, redeemed a widow named Ruth, hung out with three boys in a fiery furnace, and called a man named Nehemiah into an outrageous adventure of building a wall around a city. Aristotle was vastly more intelligent than I. But as far as I know, he didn't have the benefit of sitting down with God's self-revelation, hearing God's voice, or awakening into God's awe-inspiring creativity.

Moment by moment, our awareness of God's creativity and proximity either battens down or unleashes the floodgates of faith. Faith originates with the question, "*Who* is the true God?" Nothing in all of life unleashes or suffocates faith as much as our answer to this question. As you can see, I am fond of using imagery from the arts to revitalize our depth perception of God and his ongoing creative engagement in creation. I write with an acute awareness that for some readers, portraying God as an Artist is philosophically nonsensical and might even hint at emotionalism, animism, or idolatry. Many exist with a widespread aversion to associating the Creator with his creativity. Where does this resistance to embracing God's creativity come from?

Creativity in our times is identified with the arts, and during most of the last century, the arts were associated with entertainment. Entertainment was associated with escape and escape was associated with irrelevance. Translation? In popular society, the arts have been largely seen as irrelevant. To refer to God as *the* Artist might seem to render him irrelevant. Because this assertion might be seen as debatable, audacious, or perhaps even offensive for some, I will attempt to explain.

What role is the artist meant to play in human societies? My answer to that question differs significantly from popular thinking. I do not mean to imply that throwing a pot, planting gardenias, patching together a quilt, preparing a casserole, or redecorating a home is a silly waste of time. In fact, I believe the opposite. Buried at the core of the creative act is the creative spirit, which the Creator infuses into his image bearers. We see the evidence of this every day. Whether we are hanging a picture on a wall, designing a website, drawing a map, or etching symbols of universal mathematical laws onto a piece of paper, every one of us has been created with an internal need to create beauty and unveil meaning in our environments. Every tribe and culture evidences the predisposition to create. Like all of God's gifts, this creative spirit is distributed unevenly, being entrusted to some individuals more than others. Certain people exude creativity. From a young age, they are identified as artists. Is this random coincidence, or does God create artists for any specific purpose?

In my understanding, the artist is created by God to thrive in a vital role in society. By nature, the artist is called by God to create, cultivate, and lead human cultures. Through storytelling and imagery, he or she is meant to articulate and clarify transcendent truth in ways that lift humanity closer to the dreams God has always had for his creation. The artist is gifted with the ability to interpret events, inspire hope in moments of despair, confront hypocrisy, expose the systems and power structures that enslave humanity, and unveil existent meanings and purposes intrinsic in all reality.

How does this happen? As the artist walks with God, he experiences the beauty of God, or what is otherwise called truth. The artistic mind has been created to rise higher and soar deeper into reality. Having tasted God's beauty, the artist's soul is graced with God's dreams for humanity. The artist creates as a response to meeting, knowing, listening to, and being enraptured by God. As the artist considers his world, he is intimately aware of human depravity and does not pretend away the conditions of the unredeemed soul. The artist lives in fusion. The creative act is a translation of God's beauty and truth into symbols and stories that awaken our minds and ultimately set our hearts free. Through the creative gift, the artist exposes us to our deepest,

most firmly entrenched delusions. For an artist who is expressing herself in alignment with God, creativity is the vital force
by which humanity is drawn from despair into hope, and from
darkness into light.

At its core, the role of the artist in society is prophetic. As I
became aware of the relationship between the creative and the
prophetic, artists began popping up and waving to me from within
the pages of Scripture. A prophet warned the apostle Paul of the
danger of going to Jerusalem. Did the man simply clear his throat
and explain his concerns to Paul? No, an artist wouldn't dream
of communicating with such threadbare monotony. Instead, he
created an unforgettable work of art, binding himself with Paul's
belt to create a visual image of what the Spirit of God was saying
through him.[11] Consider Jesus and his love for parables. A par-
able is a work of art that translates transcendent truth into the
ordinary. Jesus wraps truth around mundane imagery of mustard
seeds, pearls, fishing nets, and the yeast that causes loaves of bread
to expand as they bake in the oven.

Hosea didn't just tell others that God is love. His very life
became a work of art, powerfully demonstrating God's passion for
his unfaithful bride. Then there's Jeremiah, the most bohemian of
all prophets. Jeremiah doesn't just say, "Friends and countrymen,
God is really upset with the way things are going." Even now
as I pick up my Bible and peruse what Jeremiah saw and heard,
I am bombarded with images and parables as if I were running
through the halls of an art museum. Within the first five minutes
of reading, I am confronted by an almond tree, a boiling pot, a
fortified city, an iron pillar, a bronze wall, a spring of living water,
broken cisterns, shaved heads, a wild donkey sniffing the wind, a
prostitute surrounded by her lovers, a nomad in the desert, a lion

coming out of his lair, the shriek of a woman in labor, a prowling wolf, a leopard, and a herd of snorting, pawing stallions. Through the creativity of the artist, God reveals himself by branding time-less images into the soul. They penetrate us, shake us from our slumber, and open our eyes to see and experience his glory.

A few years back, I began to assemble a group of local artists to open a creative arts ministry here in Indonesia. We began to get to know each other and started dreaming about the varied possibilities. It quickly became apparent that my friends' creative talents were remarkable. One could act, write, and perform music effortlessly. Several others were painters, sketchers, and designers with many years of experience. They could unleash tantalizing works of art onto their canvases with surprising alacrity. Another was a writer who had already published his first novel. Yet as I began to talk about merging our talents to change the world, my friends seemed paralyzed. They weren't angry or irritated. Their faces simply showed puzzlement, as if no one had ever explained to them that their Creator had ultimately gifted them for his own purposes. They reluctantly agreed to come along for the ride. Before too long, we had begun to publish a magazine, create vari-ous films, and delve into computerized animation. Meanwhile, each morning we took a little time to explore the role of the art-ist from God's perspective. Slowly, our creativity was sparked and set ablaze with God's purposes.

These artists now come alongside other ministry teams, lift their dreams off of their feet, and whisk them away to another level. I would no longer consider developing two hours' worth of material for the training of Indonesian teachers without first taking it to my friends. My material may make perfect sense to me. It may be precisely what I feel my protégés need in order to thrive as teachers. Yet if I were to stand up in front of an audience and talk through my material, even the most interested participant would not last with me for more than thirty minutes. To avoid long-winded sermonizing, I simply turn the material over to artists, and they bring it to life for a room full of excited participants.

HOBBYHORSE ART ∽

In the past artists were far more embracing of their God-ordained role. Their creative gift was handled with reverence. Obviously, this changed. What happened? During the twentieth century, the artist was bulldozed by a head-on collision with human nature. Granted, all of history testifies to the darkness in the human soul. Tribes and kingdoms have tried to destroy one another for as long as we can remember. The twentieth century, though, featured human brutality on steroids. Because of mass media, humanity for the first time was exposed and confronted by our own demonic side. On a grand scale, we realized what we are all capable of becoming—a torturing, hating, warring creature that rounds our own into concentration camps and slaughters one another like flies. Consider the century of our birth. While the Nazis were gassing Jews in Auschwitz, Japanese soldiers were organizing a mass rape of over 20,000 Chinese women and girls in the city of Nanking. Over a period of six weeks, at least 260,000 civilians were shot and dumped in a river. As a conservative estimate, 200,000 women were raped in the war between East and West Pakistan. During a two-year stretch in the Soviet Union, 682,000 prisoners were shot in the head. Red Guards in communist China murdered half a million. In Cambodia 1.7

million people were slaughtered by their own government. The century's two greatest wars resulted in the deaths of sixty million.

You get the picture.

How on earth was the artist supposed to interpret these events in what is now known as "the bloodiest century"? Really, who can blame the artist for shrinking back in horror and retreating into vicarious fantasies? The point is not to blame anyone. But one thing is clear: During that century, the artist rebelled against his God-given role. We can see the result all around us. Who are today's premium artists? Madonna, Lady Gaga, Britney Spears, and so on. In my opinion, these names represent artistic depravity. The irrelevance of the artist in western culture is symbolized by the Dada movement. Dada, which means "hobbyhorse" in French, technically lasted only about seven years (1915–1922) yet lived on as one of the most influential movements in twentieth century art. Dada's legacy is the disconnection of creativity from message, meaning, and purpose. Even today, many artists are oblivious to the fact that Dada originated as an attack against the critical role artists had always played in societies. "Art for art's sake" was the slogan of the times. This is another way of saying, "expressing nothing about nothingness for no one in particular." Dadaism was originally regarded as "anti-art." It made nonsense out of creativity. The declared purpose of Dada was to "make clear to the public at large that all established values, moral or aesthetic, had been rendered meaningless by the catastrophe of the Great War."[12]

The fruit of this movement was a century that produced some of the silliest, most juvenile art that any era in any civilization has ever known. Creative expression became impotent, emaciated, and virtually incapable of answering the deeper longings of the human spirit. People came home from work then rushed off to the arenas of artistry, where delinquent children with grown-up toys abused their liberty to tantalize our souls. They teased our imaginations with creativity that made us laugh, scared us to death, or left us running for a cold shower. We got all stirred up about nothing, then came home feeling even emptier than the day before. Artists created with no radical standards by which their expressions were judged, resulting in art that stimulated nothing more than a passing glance followed by a bewildered expression.

Society formed a dull opinion of creativity, then relegated the artist to the irrelevant fringe. Mainstream society, which once revered artists, began to perceive them as delusional. Even now, the last thing most fathers want to hear their children say is, "Dad, when I grow up, I want to be an artist!" From the perspective of more parents than we'd care to admit, dreaming of becoming an artist is like purchasing a ticket to oblivion.

Of course this isn't always the case, as a smattering of leading artists have created some breathtaking art in our times. Films such as *Life is Beautiful*, *Taare Zameen Par*, and *Braveheart* revealed the power of creativity to inspire courage, and even to change the way society thinks. In the 1970s the television show *All in the Family* brilliantly confronted America's deep-seated racial prejudice. The show captivated America by capturing the raw tension between counter cultural activists and their parents. Starring Carroll O'Connor as Archie Bunker, *All in the Family* forged new ground. Bunker's sneers and bigoted comments generated raucous laughter in millions of American living rooms. He called people "fags" and "wops" and repeatedly told his wife, Edith, to "stifle" herself. In each episode, Bunker's attempts to defend his attitudes are exposed as absurd buffoonery. Society got the message. After six years on top of television, *All in the Family* had leveled a powerful blow against misogynist and prejudiced elements in American society. Frankly, Archie Bunker accomplished what no civil rights activist had been able to accomplish. He had snuck through the back doors of America and struck racism at its heart, causing millions of Americans to begin seeing racists as fools. The genius of the show goes even deeper. *All in the Family* featured Bunker's son-in-law, a hippie college student named Michael Stivic, played by Rob Reiner, whose own form of empty idealism is repeatedly exposed as fraudulent. In other words, *All in the Family* was the first television show without a protagonist. The point was to show that every member of the family needs help.

Frankly, these works of art were an anomaly. I suspect that someday art historians will regard the twentieth century as the Dark Ages of creative expression. It will be written that, for the most part, the dignity of creativity was gutted, strangled and left to die on the irrelevant fringe of human existence. Creative expressions were reduced to capsules of escape. Even now, they sit well on the arms of vacation beach chairs as vacationers get a tan, yet they have very little to do with reality anymore. Words like *artist*, *creativity*, and *imagination* are meant to be some of the most virtuous, dignified, and noble words ever spoken. Yet they have been hijacked by a silly, meaningless creativity that has the audacity to keep us sitting in dark theaters for two wasted hours.

I suspect that the resentment of humanity runs even deeper than that. Our depravity of expression drained the Spirit from our overly structured and institutionalized lives. People feel betrayed. Where have all the inspired prophets gone when we have so deeply needed them to challenge us, to give us hope, and to fill our souls with courage to face another day? We are starving for creative leadership. Our souls are crying out for someone to speak to our deepest dungeons of confusion and darkness, to connect us with some deeper meaning, some higher purpose, and to offer us a reason to wake up and get out of bed.

When I was still an impressionable kid, the band Van Halen was all the rage. The singer's name was David Lee Roth, and in his songwriting prime, he penned one of the deepest questions ever to grace a rock 'n' roll song: "Whaddaya think the teacher's gonna look like this year?"[13] Roth practiced martial arts and could leap into the air and do the splits like a cheerleader, causing great crowds of teenage girls to scream and swoon. Many years later, he chopped off his flowing locks of blond hair and became an anonymous New York paramedic.

When did this man create his greatest art? Was it under the bright lights at the Roxy or in someone's back yard, desperately trying to breathe oxygen into a toddler's lungs after a near drowning? Van Halen was just one more symptom of the widespread framing of creativity that defined the arts in the twentieth century.

Ralph Waldo Emerson's words have never resonated so fiercely as in the century that followed him: "And we are now men, and must accept in the highest mind the same transcendent destiny; and not minors and invalids in a protected corner, not cowards fleeing before a revolution, but guides, redeemers, and benefactors, obeying the Almighty effort, and advancing on chaos and the dark."[14] Sounding almost like an art critic, Jesus spoke against the impotence of creative expression in his own era when he said, "To what can I compare this generation? They are like children sitting in the marketplaces and calling out to others:

> We played the flute for you,
>   and you did not dance;
> we sang a dirge,
>   and you did not mourn."[15]

Artists in his time had little respect for the power of truth to bring hope to humanity. Just as in our own times, many people were telling stories, singing, dancing, and playing their instruments, yet no one seemed to be taking them any more seriously than we might perceive a day at Disneyworld.

But God is not like that. Elohim is the embodiment of a true artist. He is not expressing himself for the sake of expression. He doesn't create to titillate himself. God creates with a driving purpose. He creates with revelation. His creativity is ignited and driven by his dreams for his creation. His creativity is an act of war against evil and a relentless battle to redeem what he already owns—people like Anthony. This daunting realization must affect us at the core.

In Scripture the divine creative act is never clumsily handled. When God considers you, me, and even merciless gang bangers like Anthony, he calls out to us. He draws in our hearts. He reveals glimpses of his beauty. His imagination abounds with images that he has treasured for us since before the creation of the world. He waits at the gates of our hearts with gifts in hand. He moves to create in us, to breathe his beauty into our souls, something like a gardener responding to a stretch of wasteland or a painter responding to an empty canvas. God's creativity is unveiled so beautifully in the opening lines of the gospel of John, where John mirrors the Genesis account of creation. He writes, "In the beginning was the Word, and the Word was with God, and the Word was God.... Through him all things were made."[16] John's readers are immediately swept into the grandeur of creation. We expect a full recount of Genesis 1:1–2, and yet John is about to surprise us. He suddenly pens a stunning twist to the original creation story: "In him was life, and that life was *the light of men*."[17]

John brings the Creator of the heavens into our little world like a rocket blazing from outer space, tumbling through the stratosphere and crashing through the ceiling into our most personal zones of comfort. Not only has the maker of the stars walked on our dusty roads and wept with us at funerals, he has entered our inner darkness and become the light inside of us. Even now the Spirit continues to hover over the formless and empty void, speaking the same words of creation that he did in the beginning:

"Let there be light ... in your soul!"

The apostle Paul picks up the theme, writing that the same God who once said, "Let light shine out of darkness," now makes his light shine in our hearts.[18] Portraying God as a Craftsman, Paul writes that we are God's "workmanship."[19] To some, these portrayals of the deeply personal and intimate Creator feel audacious, perhaps even blasphemous. It was no different for many readers in the first centuries after Christ. The apostles were resolute. They had seen God face to face. Their lives had been so radically impacted and so beautifully changed by God's creativity that they refused to allow us to keep the Artist at a distance.

SPIRIT-FILLED MOMENTS ∽

In Acts we read that Barnabas and Saul were traveling together when suddenly they came face to face with a sorcerer. Luke writes that Saul was "filled with the Spirit" as he stepped forward to face the adversary.[20] From this moment forward, Saul's name is inexplicably changed to Paul. When I studied this event, I asked myself, wasn't Paul *already* filled with the Spirit? He'd been a follower of Jesus for many years! I believe the answer is yes and the answer is no. Luke writes with the assumption that there's a distinction between (1) being sealed with the Spirit, unleashing God's ebb and flow of artistry in us and resulting in bearing fruit, and (2) being filled with the Spirit during certain moments, launching us into the fray to fulfill God's chosen purposes in those moments.

Luke aligns Paul's brazen response to the sorcerer with hundreds of other moments in the Scriptures when individuals are momentarily "filled with the Spirit." Let's slow down a bit and take a careful look at the following examples of Spirit-filled moments. Try not to rush through them. Instead, soak them in, allowing them to revitalize your understanding of what it means to be filled with the Spirit. Notice the triangulation of God, one of his image bearers, and the world around that person. Also notice how these moments portray how God takes purposeful action, drawing men and women of faith into movement, shattering our mundane routines in extraordinary fashion. I have added italics for emphasis.

"The Spirit of the LORD came upon him, so that he ... *went* to war."[21] "Then the Spirit of the LORD came upon Gideon, and he *blew* a trumpet."[22] "Then the Spirit of the LORD came upon Jephthah. He ... *advanced*."[23] "The Spirit of the LORD will come upon you in power, and you will *prophesy*."[24] "The Spirit of the LORD *spoke through* me."[25] "Then the Spirit of God came upon Zechariah .... He *stood* before the people and *said* ..."[26] "The Spirit is poured upon us from on high, and the desert *becomes* a fertile field."[27] "I will put my Spirit on him and he will *bring justice* to the nations."[28]

> *The Spirit of the Sovereign LORD is on me,*
>   *because the LORD has anointed me*
>   *to preach good news to the poor.*
> *He has sent me to bind up the brokenhearted,*
>   *to proclaim freedom for the captives*
>   *and release from darkness for the prisoners.*[29]

The following Spirit-filled moments can be found in the four gospels: "It will not be you speaking, but the Spirit of your Father speaking *through* you."[30] "I will put my Spirit on him, and he will *proclaim justice* to the nations."[31] "But if I *drive out demons* by the Spirit of God, then the kingdom of God has come upon you."[32] "At once the Spirit *sent* him out into the desert."[33] "Whenever you are arrested and brought to trial, do not worry beforehand about what to say. Just *say* whatever is given you at the time, for it is not you *speaking*, but the Holy Spirit."[34] "For the Holy Spirit will teach you at that time what you should *say*."[35] "But the Counselor, the Holy Spirit, whom the Father will send in my name, will teach you all things and will *remind* you of everything I have said to you."[36] "When the Counselor comes, whom I will send to you from the Father, the Spirit of truth who goes out from the Father, he will *testify* about me."[37]

Notice that Spirit-filled moments have three elements in common: God, image bearer, world. God moves from within an image bearer to somehow imprint, transform, or confront the world around that person. From the book of Acts, "But you will *receive power* when the Holy Spirit comes on you; and you will be my witnesses in Jerusalem, and in all Judea and Samaria, and to the ends of the earth."[38] "All of them were filled with the Holy Spirit and began to *speak* in [languages of tribes scattered throughout the world] as the Spirit *enabled* them."[39] "They were all filled with the Holy Spirit and *spoke* the word of God *boldly*."[40] "The two of them, sent on their way by the Holy Spirit, *went*."[41] "And now, *compelled* by the Spirit, I am *going* to Jerusalem."[42]

Through the pages of Scripture, movements of the Spirit in and through his image bearers hold a primal, hyperimprovisational unpredictability. We can never quite box the Spirit up, pin him down, make a three-point sermon out of him, predict what he will say next, or understand why, where, and when he will take action. We find him breathing his inspirations through a craftsman named Bezalel.[43] The Spirit interprets dreams through Daniel and inspires song writing in David.[44] When Samson's body erupts with superhuman physical strength, the source of that strength is the Spirit.[45] Following the death and resurrection of Christ, on the Jewish day of Pentecost, the Spirit erupts in wind and fire, resulting in a wide-open, full-throttle display of God's presence on the streets of Jerusalem. This astounding event is linked with a wave of dreams and visions, resulting in an explosive movement of faith.[46] When seen in their totality, these moments reveal a God who comes through looking like a valiant Commander, galloping on his royal steed from one fray into another, encouraging and inspiring, guiding and marshalling his followers to accomplish his purposes. Though each Spirit-filled moment is distinct and unique, there is an end game. In his own times and ways, God is moving toward the fulfillment of the dreams he's had for his creation since before he began creating the universe. He is carrying out his will on earth as it is in heaven. Pulsating through the centuries, reserving the right to move in his own ways and chosen moments, the Spirit of the Creator is just as actively engaged in human affairs as ever.

I was passing a very relaxed afternoon at a hotel in the city of Surabaya with my friends Ben Sustar and Jim Sharp, who had just arrived from the States for a visit. A waiter approached and asked if we wanted to order drinks. We ordered lime squashes. Looking at the waiter's name tag, Jim said, "Erik, get yourself one too!"

A few minutes later, the four of us chatted as we sipped our cold drinks. Speaking Indonesian, I said to Erik, "Tell us about your dreams." I was thinking about his future. He looked at me with a momentary expression of surprise. He'd heard me say, "Tell us about your *dream.*" Erik explained he'd had a dream in which Isa had appeared to him. *Isa* is the Arabic name for Jesus. Erik is the youngest of seven children and comes from a strong Muslim family. At the time Jesus appeared in his dream, he'd never had a conversation about faith with a follower of Jesus. The next morning, Erik went out to look for a church. He found one and walked in, expecting it to be filled with people. Finding it empty, he swiped a Bible, took it home, and secretly read it from cover to cover.

The pastor of that same church now meets with Erik regularly. Erik is the only believer working at the hotel. His father and his brothers have turned their backs on him. He affirms that he is persecuted daily but that his faith only grows stronger. I wasn't surprised when Erik said, "They can argue with my words, but none of them can deny that I've changed. My old self had a violent temper. Now I'm a new person. God has filled me with his love."

Erik's story is very common. I have a friend who established a thriving church in a large Southeast Asian city simply by asking Muslims whether Isa has appeared to them in their dreams. He just gathered together everyone who said yes. He avows that about one out of every four people he asks has somehow encountered Christ in a dream. God is not a distant do-nothing. He is on the move. He is alive and creating. He is the God of new beginnings. He is the God who brings freedom and hope—and he calls each of us to become "an instrument for noble purposes, made holy, useful to the Master and prepared to do any good work."[47] Whatever forms his art may take, be assured that wherever his winds blow, there is going to be internal metamorphosis followed by an external imprint.[48]

Our lives are the stories he is writing and the canvases on which he is creating his masterpieces. His warm breath is felt on the back of our necks and absorbed into everything that we are becoming. We can no longer walk into buildings and refer to them as houses of God. We ourselves have become the Creator's dwelling places. If the Spirit lives in you, every place you walk becomes the Creator's canvas. Faith is the flash point between God's creativity and your participation in his creativity. It will affect everything, exploding within you as the creativity of God descends from heaven into your heart and invades your fluctuating circumstances. Faith unleashes our talents, breathes life into our marriages, awakens beauty, changes attitudes, and sets us free to love others.

Do you want faith that burns like fire in your soul? Do you crave a faith that overcomes the world? Dare to get to know your Creator. Spend some time with the One who spoke the worlds into existence. Absorb him into your personal caverns of emptiness and confusion. Open up your soul and let the winds of his Spirit rush into you. Allow yourself to be caught in the universe's most staggering paradox. Invite Gott to become your Immanuel.

CHAPTER 4

AGONIZE
STIRRING FROM PARALYSIS

Misi Parish was twenty-four years old when she moved to the island of Papua, Indonesia. She caught her breath when she stepped off of the airplane: *This has to be one of the most beautiful places on earth.* She looked up at lush jungles carpeting Mount Cyclops, which towered majestically into the clouds. Her eyes traced the white rapids of a river streaming down the side of the mountain and through the rain forest, tumbling off a massive cliff, and falling over three hundred feet before disappearing into the sweeping green valley. To her right were rolling yellow foothills that melted into sparkling Lake Sentani. Around the lake were red dirt cliffs and dark green bluffs. Somewhere on the other side of those cliffs was the small town of Abepura, where Misi would move in with a couple named Dayu and Helena.

Misi was exuberant. But she would learn that even such beauty has both a skin and a soul. And she soon came face to face with the soul of Papua. Hours later, as Misi was unpacking her suitcase, she heard scuffling and shouting outside of her bedroom window. She ran out onto the balcony, and there below her were two gangs of teenagers rushing at one another, with several of the teens brandishing machetes. Within minutes, the gangs disappeared into the dark alleys. As she ran out to help the wounded, she thought, *Lord, where did you bring me?*

The next week Misi began her new job as a teacher. In the evenings, she went out into the streets of Abepura to look into the eyes of the people, especially the children. She was terrified by what she saw—hopelessness, drunkenness, addiction, and prostitution—yet her heart was torn open. Now as she thinks back to those first few weeks she says, "I saw their bare feet and their dyed hair. I saw eight-year-olds smoking. They were a motley-looking crew of kids. Love fell into my heart!"

Misi began asking God to show her how she might make a difference in this place. She would quickly discover that the Spirit had been ready and waiting to unleash his artistry through her into this very situation. He began prompting her to go and speak to certain kids. He began drawing her into the realm of the impossible. It wasn't long before Misi had set up "The Studio." It was a house where homeless children and teenagers could come to get a night's rest. Soon Misi had anywhere between fifteen and thirty kids sleeping at the house. It was chaotic and it was dangerous, but Misi was undeterred.

In the months that followed, Misi learned to see the Spirit rising within her in desperate circumstances. She even began to crave the terrifying moments when she would see God lighting up the darkness. She learned to let go of her safety harnesses, knowing that God would help her climb higher than ever before. Misi quickly realized that she didn't have enough money to feed her new family, but her mind was brimming with ideas. One was to teach the children how to bake and decorate cakes, then sell the cakes to generate income. She solicited support and began other small-business ventures as well. Through all these channels, the kids made about $200 a month. Soon there was enough food for everyone.

Each morning Misi woke up early and prayed, "Thank you, God, for letting me be here. I love you, and I desperately need to hear from you. Unless you show up today, I'm *toast*. Tell me, Lord, how much you love me." Then before she went off to teach, Misi gathered the kids for prayer. She taught them how to worship and how to invite God to speak to them and then to wait in silence for his gentle voice. Eventually, there were many more kids coming to their cell group. Within a year there were fifteen baptized believers who would mature into strong, fruit-bearing followers of Jesus.

Misi's life is salted with unexpected turns, mysterious surprises, and wild adventures. God carries her on his wings through every storm. She is living evidence that there is a way to find yourself, if you dare. There is a pleasure in the soul that overrides all the extreme sports we can think up, and Misi is thriving in the midst of it. This pleasure has nothing to do with leaping from an airplane with a parachute, skiing down a double-black-diamond slope, or even spending the entire day watching old reruns of *As the World Turns*. God doesn't call us to watch the world turn. He empowers us to overcome the world. People like Misi demonstrate the vast possibilities of faith lived at the edge. She not only responds to people in desperate need but prevails against the weight of the world collapsing down on them.

I'll be the first to admit that, as I churn through my schedule, the life Misi leads can feel like a distant mirage. By faith others have conquered kingdoms,[1] but I forgot to buy milk, and I have to make another run to the grocery store. Others through faith administer justice, but my kids are fighting in the backseat, and one of them has to find a bathroom fast. Somewhere at the end of a rainbow, a very lucky person might have faith that shuts the mouths of lions, but, oh, I almost forgot about that church committee meeting tonight!

Is it really possible for me to rise up tomorrow morning and walk through my entire day listening and responding to the Spirit of God? Is it possible for you, in your context, to encounter your own challenges and opportunities with the faith of people like Misi Parish? Yes. That's precisely how God created you and me to live. Wherever you are, faith can rise inside of one decision. Faith devoid of response is delusion. The Scriptures never portray faith as incidental. Faith is agonizing, and this is why faith is so rare. Lives change in the moments people surrender to the realization that faith apart from agony does not exist. The leap of faith is a battle of the will. Am I advocating a salvation by works? Am I setting Christianity back five centuries by saying that we must scratch and claw our way to eternal life? No, but know this: Jesus looked straight into the eyes of people just like you and me, and he said, "Your faith has saved you; go in peace;" "Rise and go; your faith has made you well;" "According to your faith will it be done to you;" "Go ... your faith has healed you;" "Woman, you have great faith! Your request is granted."[2]

This kind of faith, *actual* faith, the faith that Jesus commended begins in the realization that all of us are challenged and battered by an unrelenting series of skirmishes between God's transforming work in us and our addiction to our pathetic physical capabilities. These battles take place at an intensely personal level. Victory is either won or lost deep down at the core of our hearts.

FACING THE IDIOTIC STARE ∽

The word *agony* is personified in the Dutch painter Vincent van Gogh. For many artists, this man lives on as more than a well-known Post-Impressionist. He's more like a patriarch. As much as Einstein means to NASA scientists or Frank Lloyd Wright means to architects, van Gogh means to drifting, free-spirited Bohemians. Something about him helps artists understand why we've always felt so different from the crowd. Van Gogh lived with a naked soul, confronting pretension with a brazenness that still makes the rest of us clear our throats and shift uneasily in our chairs.

Van Gogh's genius was not recognized until long after his death. By all accounts, he saw himself as a miserable failure. He spent most of his life fantasizing about being a minister like his father, but the church leadership considered him unstable and erratic and never took him seriously. Like many others who could hardly endure the excruciating boredom of seminary, he was kicked out and decided to become a missionary instead. He was commissioned to serve impoverished coal miners in Northern Holland, where neighbors would hear him crying out to God in the middle of the night. After his superiors discovered that he slept on straw and refused to eat any more than the scanty diet of the miners around him, they recalled him for "undermining the dignity of the priesthood." At thirty van Gogh finally found his passion, becoming so enraptured with painting that he could do and think of almost nothing else. Later in life, he became infamous for cutting off part of his own ear during an epileptic seizure. He sold only one painting during his lifetime. At the age of thirty-seven, he wandered into a field and shot himself. Reportedly, his dying words were spoken in French, "*La tristesse durera toujours*": "The sadness will last forever."

Not only did van Gogh paint tantalizing images of the wandering soul, he also left us with hundreds of letters to his brother Theo. One Saturday morning, I was lazily drifting through this mad artist's intriguing life, when my heart was suddenly snatched up by his words. Something about his insight lit up my soul and exposed my internal paralysis. He seemed to be comparing me and my reserved, constrained manner to a painter's confrontation with his canvas. He was defying me to admit that I tend to hold God at arm's length, living with a detached stare even while greater men rise up and activate the faith to respond.

He wrote,

> Just slap anything on when you see a blank canvas staring you in the face like some imbecile. You don't know how paralyzing that is, that stare of a blank canvas is, which says to the painter, 'You can't do a thing.' The canvas has an idiotic stare and mesmerizes some painters so much that they turn into idiots themselves. Many painters are afraid in front of the blank canvas, but the blank canvas is afraid of the real, passionate painter who dares and who has broken the spell of "you can't" once and for all.[3]

Get off my back, Vincent. I have no trouble with my canvas. But the artist buried in my soul wouldn't let me off that easily. Van Gogh's words were striking a little too close to my heart. *What is this sickness in me?* I call it creative lethargy. Creative lethargy is a suffocating vacuum that smothers passion and innovation. It negates opportunities. This sickness bleeds my imagination dry and isolates me from the suffering of those around me. Creative paralysis drains my soul of God's dreams, strangling the power within me to rise and create in response to chaos, to generate order out of formlessness, and to be God's voice of hope in my world. Under its crushing weight, I am faced with the constant pressure to cave under the waves that pummel my life and tempt me to shrink away. I want to believe that adversity holds no "spell of 'you can't'" over me. I acknowledge that God holds out a living faith for me today, and I'd sure love to experience the improvisational freedom that Misi enjoys. But my life feels like "one step forward, two steps back."

Van Gogh was not finished. He continued,

> Life itself, too, is forever turning an infinitely vacant, dispiriting blank side toward man on which nothing appears, any more than it does on a blank canvas. But no matter how vacant and vain, how dead life may appear to be, the man of faith, of energy, of warmth, who knows something, will not be put off so easily. He wades in and does something and stays with it, in short, he violates, "defiles" they say. Let them talk, those cold theologians.[4]

Ah, Vincent, that's easy for you to say, but I am not so prolific. I am rather more like an artist who picks up my palette and blends my paints. I lift my brush and approach my canvas. Yet I am confronted by that idiotic stare. My heart is caught by doubts. I wonder, *Do I really have permission to call the world around me my canvas? Do I have the freedom, the audacity, the creativity, and the imagination to wade in and create on that canvas? Or am I nothing more than a detached observer?*

READ ALL ABOUT IT ∽

In the summer of my twelfth birthday, my brother Shannon and I worked for Mrs. Neilson. We rode our bikes over to her mansion covered with a thousand strips of faded pink paint trying to escape from the walls. Our purpose was to clean up her yard, and she always paid well. The front door was permanently bolted and rusted shut, and she had long ago lost the key. With each visit, we went around back, winding our way through the weeds and over the broken cement driveway. We carefully knocked on the back door, which was sagging precariously on only two hinges. Mrs. Neilson came outside and instructed us to rake her leaves and chop her weeds.

I was happy to do the work for Mrs. Neilson simply to see inside her mysterious house. Inside was a world so interesting as to be almost unbelievable. After several hours of raking, trimming, and mowing, we heard her voice calling us in for a glass of room-temperature Coke. I'd look at Shannon, and we'd brace ourselves, as if we were about to enter a broken fun house. As we entered the kitchen, we had to step carefully. Most of the floor boards were either broken in two or were missing altogether, and we saw right down onto the dirt. Every cranny held treasures: spoons and trinkets, stained coffee mugs, brown faded magazines, and corroded dishes.

The view beyond the kitchen was worth every hour of work. From floor to ceiling, we saw dozens of stacks of newspapers. The entire living room was filled up to the ceiling with the *Pasadena Star News*. Mrs. Neilson had left one narrow path between the piles for herself to squeeze through. I longed to wind my way through that path and explore upstairs to see what other surprises awaited there. We stood in amazed silence, trying to imagine how many decades it took to accumulate so many newspapers. When Mrs. Neilson disappeared into her little aisle between the piles, I wondered aloud how rich she would become the day she would take her loot to a newspaper drive. She was standing in the midst of a fortune. *And so much information at her fingertips!*

Mrs. Neilson was willing to pay a couple of boys to pull the weeds outside of her house, yet the "idiotic stare" van Gogh wrote about was within, pressing right into her internal living space. She didn't seem to see the ocean of newspapers inside her house. Day after day, year after year, those piles had grown taller and had pressed in on her freedom until she could only squeeze herself from the kitchen to the stairs. After one pile reached too high for her to stack more, she would start a new pile. Somehow it never seemed to cross her mind to ask Shannon and me to take those thousands of newspapers out and throw them away.

CONFESSIONS ∽

Now, as a grownup, I face my own stacks of newspapers and over-grown yard of weeds just outside my window. After all, the world around me is rife with oppressive conditions that are far more serious than piles of newspapers. All I have to do is look at the newspaper. While I trudge through my allotted days on this earth, 14,000 people are being infected with HIV every day. About a million people still die every year from malaria. Forty percent of America's children now live separately from their own fathers. In Eastern Europe and Russia, an estimated 900,000 abandoned or orphaned children can't remember what it feels like to hear their mothers' voices. Tucked into the heart of every major American city are sprawling, bullet-ridden war zones. Prisons are more crowded than ever before in our nation's history. So many eyes are filled with a silent cry for help.

Several years ago, I was sitting behind the wheel of my car, inching through a narrow, bustling alley of a crowded market-place, when I noticed a commotion in the distance. Through the crowd, I saw a man dragging a young woman along by the hair. He stopped and slapped her viciously. She fell to the ground. Her eyes laced with panic, she screamed for help. Instinctively, I knew I should do something. I unbuckled my seat belt, but then I began to think rationally. I realized that if I jumped out of my car, the drivers behind me would grow impatient. The street would erupt with blasting horns and hot-tempered shouts.

For one dreadful moment, which stretched far too long, a battle erupted in my heart. Should I respond or look the other way? By the time I decided that I *really* should do something, the woman was shoved into a sedan and whisked away.

The incident was yet another reminder of my inability to rise up in response to the needs around me. Creative lethargy was lurking in my soul. I was engaged in battle with my world and the world was winning. The feeling was deeper than introspection, laziness, or simple burnout. I watched how other guys would splash around in the pool with their kids while I sat in my chair at a safe distance, browsing through a book. Several of my friends made a habit of surprising their wives with flowers. One in particular would pick up the phone and call a babysitter so he could kidnap his wife for a relaxing weekend getaway together. In church I noticed how others worshiped God with unrestrained delight. I thought about a married couple who had joyfully taught Sunday school for years. Yet my own soul was stuck in neutral, needing a change of oil.

This sickness was impeding my dreams to open transformational Christian schools for Indonesian children. When I considered the challenges, pressures, and human needs all around me, I felt overwhelmed. My initiative was near standstill. Frustration began to build in my heart against the very people I was called to love and serve. Many of them seemed to think differently and to live with differing values. Walking out of my front door in the morning felt like wading into a sea of insurmountable problems.

I wanted to make excuses, reverting to a fatalistic mindset and settling for a safe and remote religious philosophy of life that had very little to do with my depth of engagement with my world. Meanwhile, Jesus began irritating me. He was becoming more difficult to read, and his words often seemed unrealistic. I was weary, and I longed for that rest he described. I wanted him to soothe my soul with comforting words.

Instead, Jesus wanted nothing to do with my resigned, cynical response to my internal paralysis. Three separate times Jesus was asked, "What must I do to inherit eternal life?" His answers surprised me. Take up your cross and follow me. Love your neighbor as yourself. Sell everything you have and give it to the poor.[5] Jesus' words are irrefutably clear: To be filled with the Spirit always results in a transformed and transforming life.

There's the catch.

God's *Spirit* ... God created me to respond to the broken and fallen conditions in my world. He calls me to be a man who is defined by action. He sets me free to breathe life into the blank stare of an empty soul. Moment by moment, the Spirit in us waits patiently for us to recognize our powerlessness apart from him. The agony of faith is not digging up the initiative to slap paint onto a canvas. It is stepping out beyond the edge of human capabilities and trusting God's Spirit to lift us into his dreams. Jesus said, "Take heart! I *have* overcome the world."[6] If you remember nothing else from this book, remember this: the agony of faith is wrenching ourselves free of prideful self reliance and crying out for the resurrected Christ to be our strength. Forge this truth into your soul, engrave it in your faith. God relentlessly places opportunities before us to fall upon our knees and invite him to breathe *his* resurrection power into us.

Far into the outback of Wyoming lies one of the Creator's most inspiring works of art. Deep in the invisible heart of the earth, there is a mysterious place where a cauldron begins to stir. The internal pressure builds until suddenly an inverted avalanche of water bursts up like a roaring rocket. The silence of the fog is overpowered and replaced by a victorious eruption in defiance of gravity and reason. As I stood at a distance, watching that water rise into the sky, the source and method of its power evaded my everyday logic. For me, Old Faithful just might be our planet's greatest metaphor of a watered and thriving soul.

A thriving soul defies logic. Your soul cannot be fed or watered by anything but the Spirit of God. To thrive is to experience the upsurge of the Spirit of Christ from the core of our being, and to live from the inside out. To be filled with the Spirit is to be vitalized, set free and moved in response to the passions of God's heart. It is inevitable that our bodies will eventually grow tired, weary, wrinkled, and become eroded by the winds of time. Yet our souls are created to be renewed, to rise up in the power of life with each new morning. God plants newer, purer treasures inside of us. As those living treasures rise up from within our souls, we embark on a journey into freedom.

Only God can move any person to respond by overflowing like a mighty river to bring healing water to the deserts around us. Jesus says, "Trust me, my child. '*My grace is sufficient for you, for my power is made perfect in weakness.*'[7] I will be your strength. I will put my words in your mouth. Step out of your sheltered structure onto the crashing waves around you, but don't take your eyes off of me. I will carry you through the storm." God is calling us to humble ourselves, so that our faith "might not rest on men's wisdom, but on God's power."[8]

GROWING YOUNG ∽

As a follower of Jesus Christ, who rose up from death in victory, I am inspired by any person who lives with the courage to crush yesterday's barriers. I was recently inspired by a picture of Michael Phelps the moment after he shattered the world record in the 100 meter butterfly in Rome. The headline reads, "Fire in the Water." Phelps is bursting up from the water in victory. Having just torn his goggles from his face, his hands are lifted to the sky in celebration. The camera captures an exultant, tenacious determination in the swimmer's fierce eyes. At some point, this Olympic champion will retire with his priceless trophies and astonishing slew of victories. He will lean back in his chair and relish the fact that he willed himself to become the fastest swimmer who ever lived. Yes, Michael Phelps will start to age. His back will start hurting and his hair will fade into white. Will he long for his youthful days when he was fire in the water?

I used to dread the thought of becoming an old man. But as my physical capabilities have begun to slow with age, I am discovering that something new is being born within. I'm actually starting to feel excited about growing old. If I ever get the chance to live so long that I walk with a cane or sit in a wheelchair, I want the moment of my death to be like the final stage of a rocket whose fire is lit on earth and explodes into the stratosphere of eternity. For this to happen, I must increasingly learn to walk in the Spirit and resist the temptation to limit my possibilities to the boundaries of my physical strength or even mental abilities. God once revealed a vision through a prophet named Zechariah, saying, "Not by might nor by power, but by my Spirit."[9] As I grow older, I'm only beginning to grasp the beauty and depth of these words. Faith opens the way for the Spirit to move in us, even as our physical might and natural power begin to melt away. Year by year, as my hair thins and changes color, the Creator will never cease to breathe his art through me. I know more than a few wrinkled men and women whose physical capabilities have withered up, yet their spiritual power grows ever more radiant. One man in particular demonstrated to me how the Spirit surges forward to create in spite of our physical enervation.

I was seventeen years old and trying to ignore the cold reality that I had to start college in a few weeks. Far more important than college was getting a tan. I had just enjoyed that afternoon at Santa Monica beach, riding waves and sipping sodas from my cooler. All I wanted was to stop at In-N-Out Burger, then return to my couch, where I could sleep. Sleeping and watching pre-season football were the best parts of my summer days. But my cousin Rusty wanted me to go and meet someone named Don Milligan. Rusty could see that somewhere in my transition into manhood I had gotten myself all turned around. He knew just the person who could help.

"Who's Don Milligan?" I was skeptical.

"Well, I think you're gonna like him. He's eighty-three years old and—"

"*Eighty-three?*"

Rusty was way ahead of me. He wouldn't take no for an answer. We drove straight to San Gabriel to meet Don Milligan. Don's living room was crowded with teenagers. They all sat around and listened and laughed as he shared hilarious stories. With a crusty voice, he entertained us with tales of young people who had followed Jesus through the Great Depression. He talked about playing piano for the silent movies when he was just a boy. He described what it was like as a sixteen-year-old to survive the great influenza epidemic of 1918 that killed millions of people around the world. He reminisced about being one of the first radio preachers in Los Angeles.

Don's stories were intriguing. *Could he be real?* He had lived one amazing story after another. Each word was spoken with such love and joyful passion for life. I couldn't get enough. Eventually, in spite of fingers that had stiffened from arthritis, he did his best to bang out some ragtime on his grand piano, and it was time to go home. I waited to be the last one out of the door.

"Paul, how about coming back next week? Maybe we can get some time together." That was all it took. He had me spotted as a wandering soul in need of some attention. The next Saturday I rode my motorcycle back to Don's house. He took me into his office, and we sat down across from one another with his big mahogany desk between us. Don perched his glasses on his nose, opened his Bible and started reading aloud from "the Book of Joy, otherwise known as Philippians." Maybe with anyone else I wouldn't have lasted for ten minutes of that, but I wasn't sitting across from just anyone. I was in the presence of a Spirit-filled soul. I would come back every Saturday for more of the same.

Don lived for helping teenagers know God. Through his stories he painted pictures of what it means to be *consumed* with God. There were always kids hanging around at his house. We piled into his car and tagged along on his frequent trips to visit kids in juvenile hall. He occasionally told us to stop dressing like bums and to stop eating like slobs. Without warning his raspy old voice would erupt as we reached for another bite of one of his barbecued sirloin steaks. "No lady wants to look at the top of your head when you are having dinner together!" His twinkle-eyed tirades were always followed with Don scowling mischievously, shaking his head and remarking, "*Kids* these days!"

We always loved it when Don lit into us. It was our chance to razz him right back. "Hey, Don, tell us that story again, the one about when you had dinner with George Washington!"

"*Kids* these days!"

One night I was with Don and his wife, Beryl, in a campground near Redding. I was helping them move to Grants Pass, Oregon. We were sitting at a picnic table next to his camper trailer. The night was clear, and, after living in smoggy LA, I had forgotten how spectacular a starry night could be. Don asked me if he could pray for me. I nodded, but I was thinking something like, *Sure, okay, but please make it fast 'cause I'm tired.*

Don asked if I wouldn't mind kneeling with him. I immediately regretted it. I was wearing shorts, and my knees were pressing into a litter of jagged pebbles. I was no longer thinking about stars. Don began to pray for me. For a while all I was thinking about was my knees. I was sure they would be bleeding when I was finally set free from this torture, but then Don's words began to sink into my soul. I had never heard a person pray quite like Don did that night. Soon his prayers melted into anguished sobs and cries. He placed his hands on my head and my shoulders, and he wept for me. I heard him prophesying that God had created me to be a spiritual leader, to be a warrior for God like David in God's kingdom.

Me? A spiritual leader? Yeah right. My hopes and dreams for life had deteriorated to a slow crawl in recent months. I had come within danger of not even graduating from high school. Our vice principal had called me into his office a few weeks before graduation. "Paul, somehow I overlooked the fact that in four years at this high school, you have not completed your required math courses. Your grades are terrible. Now I am faced with a choice: to either graduate you or not. I don't want this to wreck your future, Paul; you're a pretty good kid. But I sure hope you start to make some better choices."

I breathed a sigh of relief as I walked out of his office. But that meeting was just another confirmation that I was born for mediocrity. The world was far too heavy and confusing for me to have dreams. I could forget about achieving much of anything. The far end of my ambitions was to make enough cash to buy a 4x4 so I could tow a Jet Ski down to Mexico and camp by the beach. But here, kneeling next to me, was a person who actually cared enough to pray for me, and he saw something within me that no one else had really seen. Even the pebbles under my knees mattered less than the seeds of my future that were being awakened in my soul.

The words pouring out of Don's mouth changed my future. For the next decade, until the day he died, Don watered my soul with life, hope, and vision. Several times every year I drove my sun-roofed VW bug up the interstate to Oregon to get watered with a few more splashes. He persistently saw more in me than I was able to see within myself. His words awakened a stunning new vision in my consciousness. It was during that decade that I began to be set free from my boxed-in vision for my future and awakened into brighter dreams. My heart was alive. My mind was hungry. New emotions and curiosity began to stir and rise up within me. The university classroom became an excuse to search for hidden gems of truth. For the first time I began to experience joy and fulfillment through learning.

Don Milligan walked with an arthritic limp. When I met him, he was living in the age of thin hair and withered skin, when most others retreat quietly into the final chapter of their lives. And yet simply because the Spirit lived within him and overflowed with abundant life in his soul, Don watered seeds of life in my soul that would much later grow and burst forth as a new creation within me. Don's creative freedom had nothing to do with originality, good looks, athletic prowess, or charisma. It was simply his daily decision to live in fusion, allowing God to create through him.

THE AGONY OF PRAYER ∽

When God gave me the dream to impact the world through Christian education, he also brought together an amazing group of people, including pragmatic realists and idealistic dreamers. God knows we all need straight talk from number crunchers, at least once in a while. One morning my friend Mark popped his head into my office. "Paul, to open the kind of school we've been talking about, you are going to need to go back to the States and raise about $250,000." Mark's way of stating this without even blinking caught me off guard. The costs involved were way beyond what I had anticipated.

Six months later, I brought my family back home to California and began searching for ways to raise funds. I visited Bible studies and tried to garner invitations to speak at churches. I even opened up the phone book and called church offices. Week after week, I shared the dream God had given us with anyone who would listen. After two months of this drudgery, one man named Stan Fong had given one gift. To this day, I thank the Lord for Stan's generosity. But I was confused. God's calling on this venture was irrefutably clear, yet every door seemed to be closed and locked.

Meanwhile, I had taken on the task of memorizing Paul's letter to the Colossians. Something always happens in me when I go beyond briefly reading or casually meditating on God's Word. To infuse longer passages of Scripture into my brain, I must churn through the words and sentences over and over. My understanding then begins to sink far more deeply into the thinking of the person who originally wrote it.

I began to imagine myself sitting with Paul in a Roman prison. Even as he writes, his hands are bound to clanking chains.[10] Day after day, Paul's freedom was restricted. This was no easier for him than it would be for you or me. How he must have longed to go outside, to feel the sun on his face and to walk the streets. How he must have wanted to travel and meet the new followers of Christ living in Colossae. Instead, he was chained down, bound under the idiotic stare of four prison walls, and his internal desperation was rising. I, too, felt bound and chained in my own way. Here I was, with God's dreams bursting out from within my heart, yet my own frustration was mounting. Had God really called me into a journey that I was willing to give my life for, then disappeared?

Why, I asked myself, *isn't he forging the way?*

Paul, though, was not angry with God, nor was he pounding his fist against the walls of his jail cell. Instead, he wrote, "Since the day we heard about you, we have not stopped praying for you."[11] Paul was physically trapped. He was chained like an aging man is chained to a creaky, arthritic body. Paul was boxed in, just as anyone who rolls the dice on physical and mental capabilities is always fated to be walled in. He was pinned down like you and I can be pinned under the weight of adversity. Yet here's the crazy part: Paul was precisely where God wanted him to be, for in this state of angst, his only choice was to reach out for God's help. For those who live with a triangulated faith, prayer cannot be limited to a casual conversation with Jesus. In the convergence of heaven and earth, prayer is an agonizing struggle. Every prayer is a declaration that there is a God and we are not him. To call upon God is to experience a victorious explosion of the Spirit's passion in the soul. The word Paul uses in the same chapter to describe his struggle is the root word for *agony*. I was jolted by the realization that the agony of prayer had not been a part of my quest to create a new kind of Christian school for the developing world. My decision not to pray was a sure sign that I was taking this venture onto my own shoulders. Endeavoring to accomplish something without the agony of prayer was an act of arrogance, revealing that I believed in self-reliance more than I trusted in God.

Humbled by this realization, I stopped knocking on the doors of churches. I gave up fund raising. I stopped trying to explain my dream to others. Instead, I embraced the example of the apostle Paul and plunged myself into the battle of prayer. I told God that this dream was his, not mine. To this day, I am astonished at what happened next. Within weeks, people had begun *calling me*, asking me to come and share what God had put on my heart.

A man I had never met named Bill Deans called to ask if I would meet with him in the lobby of a hotel in Orlando. Bill was the president of Mustard Seed International (MSI), a group that helps generous donors translate their dollars into changed lives.[12] This organization searches for opportunities to assist those who would normally have no idea how to apply for a grant, especially those who pioneer in areas of dense poverty and in regions beyond the influence of Christian churches. After only a few minutes together, I knew that Bill was someone I would want to work with. Bill was a successful business owner who had devoted much of his life to ministry on behalf of the poor. Earlier in his life, Bill dedicated himself to finding ways for dozens of impoverished Eastern European children with life-threatening heart conditions to get treated by some of the world's finest doctors. Now Bill had heard about our dream to open transformational Christian schools across Indonesia and wanted to get in on the action. MSI was already involved in supporting some Christian schools and orphanages in Indonesia, India, and Taiwan and was also scoping out Sudan. Only God could have arranged such a perfect fit. To this day, the givers who have provided a large portion of the funds to open and operate the schools, orphanages, youth centers, and community education centers that we are involved with have given through MSI. Frankly, I was shocked at how quickly the tables had turned. I realized that God was *way* out ahead of me. He had already orchestrated everything for his own dreams to become a living reality. He was simply pausing, waiting patiently for me to rediscover his heart through prayer.

God's own dreamers have plenty of needs, but he has a greater number of resources. God holds direct access to several million bank accounts all across the world. He retains for himself a vast array of talented, gifted, highly skilled, and responsive people to work with. He has never given anyone a dream he won't provide for.

The point, remember, is *not* about money or fundraising. Prayer is meant to take the place of our resigned helplessness. Prayer is an internal struggle, when our anguished souls abandon physical limitations and reach up into the heart of God. Prayer is God's solution, his answer to those moments when we feel trapped and powerless to respond adequately to the pressures of life. Like Don Milligan and my friend Misi in Papua, who wakes up each morning and runs to the feet of Christ, desperately asking him to intervene in her day, I, too, have only seen lasting and genuine transformation in the world around me when I acknowledge my internal paralysis and cry out in agony for the Spirit of God to take over.

What about those smaller moments day by day when I am confronted by the idiotic stare of my own paralysis? It is in these daily episodes, when I feel frustration with a situation at work, before I stand up to speak to an audience, or when I enter into a conversation with a seeker of God, that I am learning to acknowledge my weakness and cry out in prayer for the Spirit of Christ to take over. In these moments my lips may be silent and my face may have a calm expression. But inside, my soul is ablaze, raging in the agony of prayer.

When I experience an unsettling twinge, an unsolved problem wakes me up in the night, a relationship is going south, or a situation feels insurmountable, I must recognize God's voice whispering through these situations. These moments of angst are initiated by the Holy Spirit. God himself is stirring within me, informing me that there is something out there that he deeply cares about. Moments of angst are not to be confused with collapsing in worry or drowning in fear. They are simply the Spirit's way of triggering our prayer. Through them, he informs us that it is time to find a closet and dive to our knees. With this in mind, I am convinced that those who worry all the time are simply misguided prayer warriors.

Last weekend I found myself dealing with a situation. A poor decision had been made by one of our staff members, and a lot of people were being affected. My initial impulse was a mixture of dismay and anger. There was nothing wrong with me for being stirred by this momentary twinge. It is what follows the twinge that matters. I could either collapse under dark clouds of worry and fear, resulting in a long, stressed-out, sleepless weekend that negatively affects everyone around me, or I could recognize the Spirit's voice calling me to enter the struggle of prayer. On this particular occasion, I cried out to God for help and decided to trust him to work it out. I locked my door and prayed. God responded with such grace. He flooded my heart with peace, reassuring me that he was going to take care of it. He would tell me what to say later. On Monday morning he showed me how to respond in a way that encouraged and motivated this person without leaving him feeling like a crushed and defeated failure.

MIRY CLAY ∞

One Saturday morning I woke up into a cloud of darkness. All day long I was in a mental fog. Terrible thoughts battered my mind. I was gripped by despair. I even imagined that Cyndi and our kids would be better off without me around. Every direction I turned, I kept having thoughts that I was worthless and all that my life stands for is empty and meaningless. This sudden onslaught of depression affected me physically. I could hardly even lift my hands to eat or drink. Some friends of ours needed my help to unpack a crate that had arrived from America. I couldn't even gather the energy to go help them for one hour. To make matters even more complicated, I was to speak in an Indonesian church early the next morning. But I was wiped out. I found myself unable to exert myself to prepare my talk. Exhausted, I collapsed into bed without a single thought of preparation for the next morning.

At 3:30 in the morning Someone woke me up. He was talking to me out of the darkness. He told me that he had been sent to me to instruct me to pray. I dragged myself out of bed and staggered to the toilet. I wanted to go out into the living room to pray, but I had no strength. So I lay back down in my bed. The person again told me to pray, but I answered out loud, "I can't, I have no strength to pray."

I heard him say that demons had been sent to my house on Friday night to destroy me. The reason they came was that I was going to be speaking in the pulpit of a church that was in the midst of intensive spiritual warfare. Then I was told that if I could not pray, I should just start saying "the Name." With great effort I voiced the word, "Jesus." Then I said it again and again and again. After a few minutes I sat up then stood up. As I walked around my house and prayed, a resurgent power rose up within me. Filled with the Spirit, I began praying over my family, and lifting my hands to worship God. Eventually I expelled the demons completely out of my home and commanded them in the name of Jesus never to return.

At about 4:30 that morning I sat down to prepare my talk, but God said not to prepare this time, but just to keep praying, that he would give me my message later. So eventually I went to the church and found well over three hundred people there. All through the worship, I still didn't know what I was going to say, but I was totally relaxed, even excited. I felt a sense of urgency to stand up and hear what the Spirit was going to say through me. I was introduced, and I went forward.

As I began to speak, a message came pouring out of my soul. I found that my Indonesian language was coming out more naturally and effortlessly than ever before. I was fully alive in that moment. I could see in the faces of many of the people that they had never heard this theme before, the theme that God was putting in my mouth. I found myself talking about the Consuming Fire. God is the Consuming Fire within us, awakening us. He was once the Consuming Fire on a mountain and anyone who approached that mountain had to be stoned to death. Now, though, because of the cross of Christ, the Consuming Fire burns within us. We are his hands, his feet, his heart, and even his mind. We are the body of Jesus blazing among the lost, creating his kingdom, advancing his domain of love in a broken and hurting world.

A short time after this incident, I penned these words in my journal:

> Spirit of God, come and breathe into this tired soul. Flow like a river through me. Burst out from my innermost being, stream through my mind, strengthen and guide my hands to create out from the visions and dreams you plant deep within me. Ignite my imagination, strengthen my expressions of courage, and shape words of hope in my mouth. Advance me as an instrument of light into the darkness of this city.

Even now, the Spirit of God is hovering above you, waiting to breathe his visions and dreams into your soul. Unleash yourself from *self*. Affirm the apostle Paul's words in your own life, "I can do everything through him who gives me strength."[13] The Spirit compels us to leave the upper rooms, the sanctuaries where we have been hiding in safety. When the wind blows and the tongues of fire ignite, we are even called away from our circles of fellowship. When the Spirit moves and when his passion blazes within us, how can we possibly remain in the upper room? We must run downstairs, burst through the door, and race into the streets where the nations are gathered.

CHAPTER 5

ASSIMILATE

INFUSED WITH LOGOS

I was belted into a creaking, timeworn rattletrap of a Boeing 737, hurtling down a remote jungle runway for takeoff on the island of Kalimantan, when suddenly I heard a loud blast in the right engine.

I wasn't surprised. Governments in the two-thirds world sometimes use so much energy staying in power that they don't have time to waste on petty inconveniences such as regulating the safety of their domestic travelers. We all breathed a sigh of relief when the pilot finally hit the brakes, bringing us to an abrupt stop just off the end of the runway. Minutes later, I looked out through my window, catching sight of two airport security guards shining flashlights into the troubled motor. They chatted for a while, obviously having no idea what to do. Soon the captain announced that he was going to try again. Thankfully, all of us lived to tell the tale.

On another flight just days later, I glanced out of my window during takeoff only to see a replica of my own airplane crumpled into a charred heap and shoved off the side of the runway. Sometimes the insides of the planes aren't any more reassuring. One time I reached up to get some air, only to find empty holes and exposed live wires where there should have been lights and air-conditioning vents. My brother Steve was once sitting near the back of a plane that was revving up for takeoff from Bandung en route to Yogya, Indonesia. There was one slight problem: No one had closed the back door. As the pilot accelerated down the runway, everyone noticed the ferocious wind whistling through the cabin. A flight attendant pounded her hand against the cockpit door, but to no avail. Two other flight attendants began screaming at each other, until one suddenly found the courage to jump out of her seat, scramble to the rear of the plane, and yank the door shut before the plane lifted off the ground.

Walking through one airport security station, I unloaded my coins, watch, and cell phone into a little dish, only to notice that the security device was actually unplugged from the wall. In spite of such harrowing experiences, one redeeming factor calms my nerves when I travel in this part of the world. Airlines provide complimentary cards instructing passengers how to pray for safety according to five different religions. They must figure that by listing all five, the odds are pretty good that at least someone's prayers will be heard.

Our family was once relaxing at cruising altitude en route to the cosmopolitan city state of Singapore, where visitors who are caught with narcotics get executed. I had far more important matters on my mind. *California Pizza Kitchen or Sizzler?* Tough decision. We don't have restaurants like that where we live. I was determined to have self-control. If I touched the mush on the tray in front of me, I'd ruin my appetite for the good stuff later.

Leaning back into my seat, I closed my eyes and drifted away, dreaming of an endless soup and salad bar.

I woke to the absence of noise. Without warning, both of the airplane's engines had suddenly gone silent. We plunged into a steep dive. The airplane shook and creaked violently as we fell hundreds of feet per second. Oxygen masks tumbled out of the ceiling. Over and over again, a robotic voice reverberated: "Prepare for emergency descent! Prepare for emergency descent!" After strapping oxygen masks on my boys and myself, I glanced around at the terrified eyes of the other passengers. We were about to die.

Cyndi happens to be a scrapbooking nut. What did she do in the final moments of her life? She grabbed her camera and snapped a picture of the kids and me! Her zeal to create family photo albums shows up at the craziest of times. I, too, felt somewhat calm in spite of the fact that my flesh was about to be incinerated in a ball of exploding gas then sink to the bottom of the ocean and merge into the food cycle.

Then I glanced at the faces of my children. Little Josiah and Stephen had the look of being strapped into a runaway roller coaster. Katie had a panicked expression, but she was trying to be brave like her mommy. I tried to calm my boys. *Could this really be happening?* Josiah's big, blue eyes were flooded with tears. *They're just babies. This can't be the moment of their death!* As we fell through the clouds, my heart erupted with an all-consuming passion for my family. Nothing else mattered but their survival. Soup and salad had been wiped off of my radar screen. My life, my salary, accomplishments, fulfillment, and even my golf handicap disappeared into irrelevance.

Minutes later the engines fired and the pilot pulled us out of that severe dive. The moment our wheels touched the pavement in Singapore, all of the passengers erupted into wild applause. We never received an explanation. As I stepped off the plane, I wanted nothing more than to be with Cyndi and my children. I wanted to hold and hug them, to look into their eyes, to laugh with them, and to keep living life with them.

HIDDEN TREASURES ∾

Later that night as I wrote in my journal, I pondered how our little crisis had affected me. Unlike the fear and paralysis that I described in the last chapter, something more virtuous had floated to the surface. All those trappings I thought I cared about had evaporated. They had been reduced to meaningless diversions, swept away by a surprisingly powerful composite of life and love that had been buried far more deeply within my soul.

In moments of truth, our souls show up fast, and they bring whatever they've got stuffed away in their pockets. I suppose that we'd all love to see the best in us rise up in moments of stress and confusion. Most of us *want* to be problem solvers, responding with words of wisdom to others while living joyful, courageous lives. Is there anyone alive who doesn't want to be a more patient partner or a more proactive parent at the end of a long, tiring day? In the last chapter, we focused on the agony of prayer, learning to cry out to God for his Spirit to move through us, bringing his hope to the world around us. Is there anything else we can do to position ourselves to become vessels of God's artistry?

Jesus answers this question. His words are clear. They go straight to the heart of the matter. "The good man brings good things out of the good stored up in his heart, and the evil man brings evil things out of the evil stored up in his heart. For out of the overflow of his heart his mouth speaks."[1] The emphasis in Jesus' statement is the phrase *stored up*. The Greek word is *thesauros*, meaning "treasure chest." This word has morphed into our English *thesaurus*, which refers to a treasure chest of words.

Jesus is saying that God has designed us to receive before we can give. Who can give away a treasure he doesn't first own? It's so simple. And yet this uncomplicated truth has been one of the most liberating realizations of my entire life. I can create something beautiful only if beauty has been stored up in my heart. I can become a voice of hope if I live with hope at my core. And love? "We love because he first loved us."[2] The apostle Paul writes that we can be a comfort to others when we ourselves have received comfort from God.[3] We will be set free to fill another person's heart with joy only when we have been lifted by the joy of the Spirit. You and I can bring peace into a chaotic environment only if we ourselves are walking in peace. Consider Paul's words in Romans 15, "May the God of hope *fill* you with all joy and peace as you trust in him, so that you may *overflow* with hope by the power of the Holy Spirit."[4]

Picture for a moment a painter standing in front of a blank canvas. Remember the van Gogh quote from the last chapter about his confrontation with the idiotic stare of the canvas? See how this painter takes up her brush and her colors. She begins to transform the canvas into a work of art. Her hand works deftly, guiding her instrument smoothly and with masterful brush strokes. Meaning, depth, energy, and beauty emerge onto the canvas. Perhaps to the casual observer, her movements feel spontaneous—the result of a whim floating on the breezes of emotion. Yet where does this work of art *really* originate? We've got to look into what is actually happening inside of the painter.

Whether it's conscious or subconscious, the painter is drawing from a vast storehouse of treasures. Her work of art reflects a lifetime of listening, watching, interpreting, honing her abilities, and discovering meaning in her world. The painting, in its finished state, is an amalgamation that calls forth experiences and observations from the painter's entire life, reaching all the way back into her childhood.

How does this happen? At the most unconstrained and everyday level of receptivity, we see and hear what's going on in our environments. We pause to consider causes and effects. We notice colors, shapes, textures, and forms juxtaposed in various combinations. Pablo Picasso described it like this: "The artist is a receptacle for emotions that come from all over the place: from the sky, from the earth, from a scrap of paper, from a passing shape, from a spider's web." Picasso's use of the word *receptacle* applies to all of us. We read books. We listen to the teachings of our pastors and teachers. We read advice columns in the newspaper. We look around and consider the aesthetics in our environments, as well as the opportunities and needs around us. As we accumulate this data, we transform it into a variety of symbols, metaphors, and ideas, storing them up within us. Our hearts naturally stir them into the expressions that rise to the surface of our souls, flooding our attitudes, words, and actions. These treasures emerge in their own time, making their own imprints beyond us.

You, too, are an artist, in the sense that the world around you is the Creator's own canvas. The hurting and lonely hearts, the hungry minds, the thirsty souls that you will encounter today are waiting for God to create through you. You are moving forward in time, encountering moments and circumstances that cry out to be redeemed. God calls each of his image bearers to walk through each day with his own primal words of creation being voiced from within, "Let there be light!" These words take on an infinite number of forms that vary according to our circumstances. As the Spirit moves through us, he draws from the treasures that have been stored up in our hearts, and he uses them to create his own works of art. Do you long to become an instrument more useful for God's purposes? Me too. The question God wants us to answer is, "What treasures are we storing up in our hearts?"

DROIDS AND IPODS

The perceptivity of children is turned up much higher than we adults often remember. We tend to forget how intimately tuned in we were as kids to the aromas floating from our mothers' kitchens, the tones in our fathers' voices, the lure of primary colors, or even the noise of a fly buzzing near the window. Whereas our own ability to assimilate data may fade over the years, our children absorb everything around them — especially television and film footage.

Nowadays my kids don't watch television on weekdays, but for a while everything revolved around *Star Wars*. Han Solo seemed to be eating at our dinner table every night. When we played Twenty Questions, my boys were easy to guess. They were always thinking of light sabers, galactic battles, spaceships, or droids. It was a surreal experience to watch *Star Wars* with my kids. Sitting on the couch next to me, they looked like a row of deactivated robots getting their batteries recharged.

We say that we *watch* television, but perhaps this word doesn't quite capture what is really happening. We can *watch* a baseball game. We *watch* the clothes tumble in the dryer at the Laundromat.

When grown men and women turn on the television, maybe we can simply watch. But children don't *ever* simply *watch*. They get synced like iPods. Their creative outflow is either trampled or set free by whatever data stream into their souls. Every scene storms through their hearts and soon begins to emerge through their words, attitudes, actions, and aspirations.

Jesus said when a disciple is fully trained, he will become like his master. Many of us grew up having spent countless hours under the tutelage of the glowing guru. Now, as parents, we must grapple with whether we want this teacher active in our children's hearts. Ever before us is the question, "As the Creator moves to create from inside the workshop of our children's hearts, what treasures will he find?" Will he choose from iridescent colors and hues, using them to paint life, hope, beauty, dignity, and grace? Or will he unearth the useless gray shades of sexual deviance, artificial religion, worship of things, arrogance, selfishness, aggression, and cynicism?

My own experiences with streaming data trace back to about the time my parents moved our family from the jungles of New Guinea into the world of cars, electric lights, and televisions. I remember sitting with my legs crossed on my grandmother's carpet, encountering the tantalizing world of television. I stared at a white guy who lived among apes and talked with elephants. I'd never heard of Tarzan before, but the film intrigued me. It was about people who lived in the jungle, so I could relate to this Tarzan. I was swept away, back into the villages where I had been raised. I observed several men dressed as lion tamers. As I recall, they wore khaki shorts and socks yanked up to their knees. Rifles were slung over their shoulders. They were marching single file along a trail near the edge of a precipitous cliff. Natives were bearing heavy wooden crates on their shoulders. Suddenly a man with a box slipped and fell off the cliff. I listened to his voice fading off of the screen. "*Aaahhhh!*" What happened next?

The others kept on marching—they didn't even turn their heads! To this day, three decades later, I can still remember the shock I felt in that moment. I had no clue about special effects, and I had never been to Universal Studios. As far as I was concerned, a jungle tragedy had reached out from the television and slapped me across the face. It was the first of many screen scenes that would claw at my dignity, ripping open wounds in my child-like faith in the powerful river of life that flows from God.

ASSIMILATION ∽

Hiding priceless treasures in our hearts, treasures that are useful to the Spirit of God, involves far more than clicking off the TV or checking the rating of a movie. We must advance beyond a passive acceptance of what we know to be true. We must get synced with the creating, living, and active expressions of the Creator. I didn't really grasp how indispensable this life principle is until I was in my early twenties. In those years I sat at the feet of a red-bearded shepherd of souls named Tom Wolf. Affectionately known as Brother Tom, this modern patriarch was a masterful communicator with an around-the-clock sense of humor. Behind his constant smile was a soul that had spent a lifetime assimilating God's truth.

One evening I was in class with Brother Tom. This was a master's-level class, and we were comparing and contrasting the Christian faith with other worldviews. He casually referred to the incident when the apostle Paul rebuked the apostle Peter publicly. We all gathered up our Bibles and waited for him to tell us the passage. He repeated, "Open to the place in the Scriptures where Paul writes of his public confrontation with Peter." We looked at each other in bewilderment. Brother Tom put down his Bible, and, for some reason, he looked straight at me. "You are preparing to advance the kingdom of God to the nations, yet none of you has any idea where in the Bible to find this story?" An awkward silence filled the room.

"Somewhere in Acts?" I guessed, trying to break the tension.

"Paul, is God's Word a *part of you*? Listen to me, bro. I am speaking to you in truth and love. You must get passionate about devouring God's Word. It must leap off of the paper into your soul. His words must become so deeply embedded within you that they are inseparable from who you are! Now let's turn to Galatians chapter 2." That rebuke still haunts me. I was so unfamiliar with the Scriptures that I couldn't even find one of the most significant apostolic moments ever recorded. Yet notice carefully: Brother Tom didn't rebuke me for not *knowing*. He went beyond mere knowledge to the state of my heart. He called me out for my failure of assimilation.

God doesn't call us to tinker around at the fringe of his words, but to become living expressions of them. Assimilation is the process of advancing from mental knowledge to internal metamorphosis. This is the inside story of actualizing our faith. God not only calls us to bear fruit, to dream impossible dreams, and to change the world, he provides us with the means to accomplish his calling. We're not talking about biblical trivia, but about God's truth that must be assimilated into our creative DNA. What we initially understand from an arm's length must become intrinsic to our very being.

Jesus related various stories using the imagery of farmers sowing their seeds. In one of them, he described various depths of receptivity to God's words.[5] He compared these divine expressions, *logos Theos*, to seeds falling onto the surface of our hearts, where they are easily snatched away. Jesus described other hearts that hear his words or even receive them joyfully, yet in the end he only commends the heart that *activates*, that secures his words and retains them through assimilation. These hearts are the ones that flourish to "bear fruit."[6]

Assimilation is vital to mastering any endeavor. When my family left the jungle and settled in Southern California, I battled to adapt myself to my new environment. Having never tasted smog before, every breath of that filthy air filled my gasping lungs with pain. The smog was so hideous that for two weeks I was completely unaware that my house was built near the base of a 5,715-foot mountain—I simply couldn't see it when I rode my new bicycle to and from school. There I was, a new kid who had been raised with the sound of cicadas in the jungle, riding a shiny silver bike through several gangs' territories on the north side of Pasadena. After my bike was stolen, I found myself walking every day, and I rarely made it home from school without a busted lip or a torn shirt.

My dad finally had enough. He sat me down in the living room and explained that neighborhood bullies hone in on fear. Kids always size one another up by the expressions in their eyes. He said that the vast majority of street fights are won or at least prevented simply by an expression of courage on one's face. Dad wasn't about to start driving me to school. He wanted me to tough this one out. But he knew that in real confrontations, few boys are good enough actors to *pretend* to have courage. This wasn't about masking my fear, but mastering it.

The next day he took me down to a karate dojo. There I was to spend my afternoons and weekends studying the art of self-defense under a sensei. Nowadays, as I look back on those early stages of mastering a martial art, I smile at the genius of assimilation. My first few weeks felt like nothing more than dancing lessons. I was forced to learn choreographed movements, putting together various combinations of blocks, punches, and kicks. Over and over, I kicked and punched into the air, without an opponent's torso in front of me to aim at. These memorized movements were an essential start. My task was to assimilate certain movements by repeating them over and over until they became my own. Day after day I learned and practiced these progressions with almost no physical contact with opponents. When I was able to prove to the sensei that I could carry out each progression, I was handed a different colored belt and moved on to sparring with a real opponent. Suddenly the blocks, punches, and kicks that I had practiced so many times naturally and effortlessly exploded from within me. The same movements that before had been a calculated mental process had now become subconscious. It was exhilarating to spar naturally, even sometimes overpowering and defeating my opponents without any planning or mental strain.

God's Word being activated in us is really no different. Our intimate relationship with the Scripture begins with listening and reading. This is why our family has God's written expressions on the walls of our kitchen, and our children repeat them at the breakfast table. We discipline ourselves to open the Scriptures, to meditate on them, and to memorize them as a consistent part of our daily routine. Each morning there is a time to be silent and unite our passions and dreams with God's heart.

As Jesus said, we must "clean the inside of the cup and dish, and then the outside also will be clean."[7] Hearing, reading, and even memorizing God's words are only the preliminary stages of assimilation. We must plant them deeper and deeper within our hearts. In time his voice rises within us. His expressions paint that inner canvas with the virtues and dreams of his own heart. His presence in our souls unites our passions with his dreams. Ultimately, his own creativity begins to overflow into our daily actions, words, attitudes, and thoughts. As we encounter moments of resistance and pressure, God's own life springs from the very core of our being, strengthening us with creative resources we could never access on our own.

I have never witnessed assimilation more clearly than in my mother's life. By the time she was eleven years old, she had memorized five hundred Bible verses to win a trip to summer camp. Then, as she blossomed into a young woman, those verses became who she was rather than what she had memorized. Throughout her life, even as she continued to hide hundreds of other Scriptures in her heart, Mom never made a habit of quoting them at people. Instead, she was bent on becoming a living expression of them. As a result, she pursued her life with an astounding level of creative freedom. For as long as I can remember, younger women would come to our house to get snippets of time with her, asking for her prayers and counsel. By the time she died of pancreatic cancer at the age of sixty-seven, she had quietly yet powerfully influenced thousands of lives.

Recently, I returned to the remote cluster of villages where I grew up. I was reunited with several of the women that Mom had led into a relationship with Jesus and mentored. These women wailed uncontrollably when they heard she had died. Through her tears, one woman said, "Your mom was my closest friend. She was an angel from heaven." Well, she got it partially right. Mom was as human as the rest of us, but there *was* eternity in her heart. Her wisdom, patience, kindness, and gentleness were God's own expressions assimilated into the life of one of his image bearers.

Mother Teresa's order, Missionaries of Charity, is today serving the poor in 122 countries. Every morning, all across the world, these women unite themselves with this prayer, "Jesus ... penetrate my being and take such hold of me that my life becomes a radiation of your own life. Give your light through me and remain in me in such a way that every soul I come in contact with can feel your presence in me. May people not see me, but see you in me."[8] Isn't that beautiful? Thankfully, we don't have to be nuns, missionaries, or pastors to become living expressions of God's Word. God calls each of us to become his instruments of creation, to enter each new day with his words abiding in us.

WHEN PUT INTO PRACTICE ∽

The Scriptures have never been meant for half-hearted intellectual speculations over combinations of words juxtaposed and inked onto parchments. Those words are meant to spring from the parchments, entering us through our eyes and ears, becoming the treasures in our souls, and bursting out to create through us. Those words are meant to assimilate the sound of God's voice and the dreams in God's heart into our own hearts. Those words are a reminder that although God cannot be seen with our eyes, he is everywhere speaking, whispering, creating, responding, and writing his stories through his image bearers. Those words are given to capture us in his love and set us free into his plans.

Jesus was the greatest teacher who ever lived. He was intent on forging wisdom in his disciples' hearts. Yet he never took his students inside a traditional classroom. He had a more compelling method of drawing them beyond cerebral learning into the Spirit-fueled life. Everything they learned was to be tested under pressure and stretched beyond the edge of impossibility. They walked across dusty roads and encountered everyone from desperate lepers to arrogant power brokers. One day they might be in a boat, tossed about on the storming sea, desperately bailing water. Another day they might be confronted by a crazed, shouting man filled with raging demons. They were witnesses to God in flesh, walking among them, leading them, comforting them, calling them, rebuking them. He was a God who shattered their culture's self-imposed limitations.

In the early stages, the disciples were to watch, listen, ask questions, and learn. Jesus wanted first to advance beyond their outer, more visible layers to begin to form stronger treasures at the core. He challenged them to examine whether their inner being could stand up against the surging, rising storms of life. And he taught them that his Logos, when put into practice, would be as trustworthy in a time of crisis as a strong structure built on a solid-rock foundation.[9]

What is this Logos?

When I began to study what the apostles actually wrote when they referred to God's Word, I realized they were thinking of something more expansive than anything I had previously imagined. *Logos* was first used by the Greek philosopher Heraclitus, who lived 600 years before Christ. It was understood by the Greeks as "the divine reason or plan which coordinates a changing universe."[10] It's worth at least a brief moment of our time to have a closer look at the Greek twin brothers *logos* and *rhema*, along with their Hebrew cousin *dabar*.[11] The Hebrew word *dabar* is used about 2,500 times in the Old Testament and takes on hundreds of forms. When translated to mean "the Word of God," it carries the essence of fruitfulness or the bringing forth of living things out of nothingness. From Isaiah,

> So shall My dabar be that goes forth from My mouth;
> It shall not return to Me void,
> But it shall accomplish what I please,
> And it shall prosper in the thing for which I sent it.[12]

In the New Testament, the author of Hebrews writes that God is "sustaining all things by his powerful [rhema]"[13] and that "the [logos] of God is living and active. Sharper than any double-edged sword, it penetrates even to dividing soul and spirit, joints and marrow; it judges the thoughts and attitudes of the heart."[14] Paul portrays the Rhema as a sword being grasped in the hand of the Spirit of God.[15] In his letter to the Colossians, he writes that the "[logos] of truth, the gospel, which has come to [literally, "penetrated into"] you, just as in all the world also it is constantly bearing fruit and increasing."[16] In 1 Thessalonians, Paul describes the "[logos] of God, which also performs its work in you who believe."[17] In another place we read, "Finally, brethren, pray for us, that the [logos] of the Lord may run swiftly."[18] As James writes of the [Logos], he chooses a word that describes a seed being inserted into the earth, then swelling and bursting up to bear fruit. The Word penetrates the soul and overflows from within to "zoopoieo," or increase life, within us and beyond us. From John we read,

I write to you, young men,
because you are strong,
and the [logos] of God lives in you,
and you have overcome the evil one. [19]

How do these portrayals compare with casual musings over the Bible from a safe distance? Alive! Active! Penetrating! Dividing! Judging! Bearing fruit in all the cosmos! Creating! Increasing life! Overcoming! Working! Racing forward! The Logos is not a handbook. The Logos is the power of God, spoken from his mouth and transforming his own dreams into a living reality.

I played for a football coach in high school who almost never raised his voice. When he spoke to our team, his voice was low, his eyes were intent, and he constantly had our full attention. We were in awe of this man. We would have jumped off a cliff for him. In college I worked as an assistant football coach for another man. This fellow would frequently scream at the kids and throw things around. He commanded no respect whatsoever. His practices wasted an immense amount of time because it always took a few minutes to get the herd of players to do what he asked.

When mere mortals raise our voices and say something is going to happen, it may or may not happen. When politicians make promises about change, circumstances may or may not change. When God speaks, the universe changes. Creation stands in awe of him. Every atom awaits his command. When God says, "Let there be light!" be assured that light will materialize, even out of nothingness. This is what it means when we say that God's words are the Logos. The words that pour out of God's mouth are the Logos Zoe, the life originating in God the

Father, spoken forth as an unstoppable creative force into the entire cosmos.

When the Logos is assimilated into our souls, it burns like fire within us and bursts forth to transform the world around us. Jeremiah related his blazing encounter with God's Word in this way,

> Then I said, "I will not make mention of Him,
> Nor speak anymore in His name."
> But His [dabar] was in my heart like a burning fire
> Shut up in my bones;
> I was weary of holding it back,
> And I could not.[20]

The flames that crackled in his bones are the same inferno of life that will burst into being within your own soul, igniting courage in the most difficult moments, words of wisdom when others are dazed and confused, love for your most unforgiveable enemy, a breakthrough idea at your staff meeting, or a gentle and gracious response to a barbed criticism.

The Spirit's on the move — strap on your seat belt! God is calling us to advance beyond Sunday morning sermons. He beckons us to rise every morning and spend time with him. He has recorded his words onto paper for you. He wants you to listen to his voice, to find his heart through his words, to infuse those words into your mind, and to consume them into your soul. It's time to "let the word of Christ dwell in you richly."[21] When you hold your Bible, you are holding a storehouse of priceless treasures. They are worth more than any amount of money you could possibly possess. Take the Bible off of your shelf. Wipe the dust off of it. Assimilate it into your life so that you can plunge into your days with unbounded freedom. With God's Word living and active in your soul, stand up and move together with others to light the darkness and breathe his life into your world.

CHAPTER 6

ANTICIPATE

NAVIGATING THE NIGHT

The pounding drums and screaming electric guitars grew louder as I carefully made my way through the dark parking lot toward the nightclub in the basement of a shopping plaza not far from my house. As I hauled open the large metal door, my ears were blasted by a wall of noise. Strobe lights flashed across the ceiling. I merged into the crowd, my eyes adjusting slowly to my surroundings. All around me were teenagers with tattooed arms, Mohawks, and black eyeliner. In the center of the crowd was the stage where the band was playing. Among the faces of the kids, I saw gang members and drugged-up addicts.

I had just entered a local church outreach. The band, at least, was worshiping Jesus. Then Pastor Raymond jumped up on the stage and began telling stories. He highlighted certain kids in the crowd who had chosen to surrender their lives to God. He was hilarious. Every few minutes he started singing in the middle of his message. Soon he was talking about the courage of Christians being fed to lions in the arenas of Rome. He told the kids that

God loved them, had created them in his own image and brought them into the world for a purpose. His words were brimming with hope, and every person listening was captivated. At the end of the message, a large number of kids raised their hands to surrender their lives to Christ. Then they were invited to join cell groups where they would be mentored.

Later that night I sat down with Pastor Raymond over two cups of coffee. Granted, if we had been in Los Angeles or London, starting a church in a nightclub might be considered old news. In Indonesia this was about as edgy as it gets. I asked, "Where did you come up with this idea?"

He said, "What do you mean?"

"You must have gone to some conference or been told about churches in nightclubs."

"No, the Holy Spirit spoke to me. God had been opening my eyes to the thousands of kids in the underworld of Indonesia. Outcasts living in the streets, disenfranchised and drugged up. Prostituted children. Rebels without a cause. Needles. AIDS. I realized those kids would never set one foot inside my church. So God told me to start a church in a club. I had to go find them. I had to enter *their* world."

Raymond's innovative way of chasing his dream raises the standard for how I, too, want to advance into my own future. I don't mean that I plan to copy his method of starting churches in nightclubs. Neither do I mean to imply that different is always better. It is the way that Raymond so freely and audaciously adapted his approach in response to God's voice that inspires me. From the start, there was no straight and visible path between Raymond and the subculture of kids he wanted to reach. Seemingly massive barriers blockaded his approach. Raymond and those kids walked the same streets yet lived in two different worlds. For others, the barriers between those worlds were perceived as unassailable.

Raymond saw the barriers differently. He was confident that if God had given him a dream to reach those kids, then God would also provide the *means* to reach them. When Raymond initially jumped into the fray, he had no idea that he would be starting an outreach in a nightclub. But he did trust that God would make a way. God was moving in front of him, arranging the elements for his own purposes. Raymond's assignment was simply to step forward and let God open his eyes to new possibilities. With faith that God would reveal each solution, Raymond was free to improvise in response to whatever God told him. He was at liberty to adapt his approach and explore various possibilities until he found a way around, over, or even directly through each barrier.

So far much of this book has centered on our response to God's voice and to his love for the world around us. We've focused our faith on a fully engaged Creator and scrapped any mental remnants of a distant and aloof God. We've honed in on the way God is moving his creation toward the fulfillment of his dreams rather than sitting and contemplating himself. We've been reminded that God created us to rise in the freedom of his Spirit and that becoming instruments of his creativity involves assimilating his living and active Word. All along we've been exploring how faith allows us to hear and respond to a God who moves from within to create his artistry in and through us. Yet does faith also augment how we see horizontally? Does the Spirit teach us how to see the world around us with a completely new vision? There's no doubt about it. Faith sets us free to see through God's eyes, exposing us to previously unnoticed possibilities in the world around us. The theme of this chapter is trusting that God is out in front both in time and space, drawing his purposes into alignment with his dreams rather than waddling clumsily behind people, trying his best to keep up.

THE MENTAL CORRIDOR ∽

As an educator for the last seventeen years, one of my roles has been to help teachers learn how to remove the barriers from around the eyes of their students, helping them to grasp previously invisible possibilities. Picture a little girl named Lucy sitting in a first grade classroom. Lucy's mind contains the intrinsic potential to envision, grasp, and apply the mathematical principles of change or what is more commonly referred to as calculus. Over the next decade or so, her mind will be slowly and carefully opened by expert teachers. She will be led through an expanding corridor of learning. One door will open after another, allowing Lucy to understand mathematics with greater vision. New layers of truth will be revealed until she is able to think fluently in the language of calculus. It is important to remember that the mathematical laws of change exist independently of this child. Calculus has existed since God called the universe into being from the primordial abyss. The laws of change constantly affect her and the environment all around her. I might even muse with a bit of poetic flair that calculus swirls around Lucy and waits patiently for her eyes to be opened. Its laws are readily available to be accessed when her mind has opened sufficiently to reach out for them. As a first grader, though, Lucy cannot see calculus even if she squints.

Being led by the Spirit of God is like this. God leads us to the edges of possibility, then calls us to take leaps of faith. Always the next leap appears insurmountable. We are tempted to shrink back, but he says, "Jump!" In my own story, each time I've stepped off another ledge, I've felt the terror of the unknown and the helplessness of falling. Yet not once has God failed to provide a place for me to touch down. I am no different than a child growing into an increasing awareness of mathematics. Each step of faith opens my vision of God a bit more and my trust in his artistry all around me grows deeper. Undoubtedly I am still only a few short steps down the long corridor. Once in a while, I turn around and consider last year's leaps of faith. Looking back, one can feel like a calculus student thinking about elementary addition and subtraction.

Can you relate? Taking a risk in response to God's voice might feel terrifying in the moment. God wants to expand your vision and to increase your faith. Be assured that for every barrier you encounter, he has already created a solution. For every cliff he tells you to jump off, there is a better path on which to run. You will find that every fall takes you to a higher place.

Educators sometimes use the word *divergent* to describe minds that more easily adapt to unfolding possibilities. The word *divergent* signifies growth, expansion, and spreading out like the branches of a tree. Highly divergent thinkers are reluctant to let their exploration of new possibilities grind to a premature ending. Like Pastor Raymond, they hunger to seek out previously unexplored opportunities for innovation and understanding. They might occasionally be heard saying words like *unlikely* or *perhaps*, yet words such as *impossible* or *unthinkable* are almost never uttered.

Imagine, for example, that a time machine takes you to a dusty road in 1700. Before too long, a wagon approaches, and you hop on board with three other passengers. As you clatter along, you decide to have some fun. *Hmm, what to talk about?* Ah, wireless technology. After a few minutes of describing how a cell phone works, you find that your new friends haven't even heard of electricity. *You* have already experienced the reality of wireless technology, but to them the concept is about as real as Jack and the Beanstalk. How divergent are their minds? One of the passengers points his finger at you and growls, "You foolish dreamer; that's *impossible!*" Then he rolls his eyes and mutters something about the ignorance of people who haven't learned how to think straight. The second man waits for a few moments, then he muses, "Aw, shucks, that's pretty farfetched, but fascinatin', indeed!" The third one slowly says, "That's beautiful ... I haven't talked to my brother in five years. Just imagine if I could listen to his voice right now!"

Thinking over the probable responses of others who lived centuries ago, it's easy for all of us to see that humanity was once unconscious of a vast number of possibilities that we now accept as normal. Yesterday's miracles have become today's trivialities. Could it be possible that even now, you and I continue to exist in a vast sea of possibility? Yes. Faith is the eye opener, helping us to break through today's barriers and rise into a way of living where innovation becomes the norm rather than the exception.

BOUNDLESS POSSIBILITIES ∾

Innovation is a word that gets thrown around a lot. It is most often associated with technology or business. What does it really mean? I define *innovation* as the discovery and actualization of a previously untapped possibility. Innovative people see the world from a different vantage point than the rest of us. They see possibilities as opportunities and snatch them up like a child with a bucket walking through a ripe strawberry patch while the rest of us are napping or sleepwalking. In much the same way, faith in God unlocks and releases our ability to walk through life picking juicy and delicious fruit from the hidden possibilities that God arranges all around us. Faith transforms the way we see *everything*.

This morning I went to the fridge and reached for a green apple. After eating it down to the core, I mindlessly tossed away enough food to feed every hungry person on the entire planet. Have I lost my marbles? Not at all. The tiny seeds hidden away in the core of that apple are now lying in the dark, trapped under the lid of a trash can. Yet even *one* of those seeds, if planted, contains the miraculous possibility of bursting up out of the soil to become an apple tree. The combined seeds in that tree would contain the possibility of an entire orchard. If the seeds in that orchard were replanted, they could possibly become thousands of other orchards, and so on. Imagine that. One apple seed lying in my trash contains the intrinsic potential to feed every hungry person on earth!

One small seed feeding billions of people describes the nature of the Spirit's artistry. God is the source and cause of life. Where there is life, one always sees metamorphosis and growth. God is a multiplier of exponential proportions. With him we are constantly at the edge of explosive possibilities. Here in Indonesia, between 1960 and 1970, approximately four million people made the decision to surrender their allegiance to Christ. That's not a typo, that's four *million*! In Sumatra, the Batak tribe killed the first few missionary families that went to live there. Did the handful of Christian martyrs who lived and died there have any idea that hundreds of thousands of Batak people would someday know and worship God in the very place where their blood soaked the ground? In the kingdom of God, a child's sacrifice of bread and fish offered to Jesus contains the possibility of feeding a vast crowd. One small step of faith in response to Jesus' voice can turn a futile night of fishing into a swarm of fish so large that nets begin to tear. Jesus made it his mission to teach his disciples to see through God's eyes. He said, "The kingdom of heaven is like a mustard seed, which a man took and planted in his field. Though it is the smallest of all your seeds, yet when it grows, it is the largest of garden plants and becomes a tree, so that the birds of the air come and perch in its branches."[1]

Yesterday I kneeled on the ground in a village. I was surrounded by a crowd of children. I handed bracelets to each child, then gave them beads to put on their bracelets. Using their language, I said, "This first bead represents our sin. Is there anyone here who has never sinned?" They all laughed. Guilty as charged. "Red is for the blood of Jesus, who died on the cross to pay for our sins and take away our shame. White is the purity in our hearts after the blood of Jesus washes through. Blue is God's river of life that flows through us. Do you see how tall and green that tree is? It must have very strong, deep roots! Green is the growth that we experience when God lives in us. Yellow stands for the streets made of gold in heaven. If God lives in your heart, you don't have to be afraid to die. Dying is like graduating to a much better place."

One simple, much too short conversation. One small seed and perhaps one trusting heart. Only God knows what he will do with that little seed. By faith I trust that he will multiply it. After all, that's his way.

While we're on the subject of possibilities, what do you think God really sees as he looks at *you*? God sees what he created you to become. After all, he designed you and created you for his own pleasure—and he always looks deeper and farther ahead. Your Maker delights in the exploration and unleashing of the possibilities he has already planted within you. Even now, he is poised to make a work of art from a damaged reputation, a divorced single dad, a high school dropout. He is drawn to the impoverished beggar, the teenager who failed Algebra I, the athlete on the sidelines, and that quiet little boy in the back of the class, scribbling pictures on his worksheet. Jesus raises the standard for innovation. He locates and awakens the hidden possibilities that only God is able to reveal. Looking out at a crowd of people who were poor, illiterate, confused, and lost, he said to them, "You are the light of the world."[2] Jesus spoke of what he saw in Nathanael's heart, "Here is a true Israelite, in whom there is nothing false."[3]

To others, Simon was an illiterate, temperamental teenage fisherman. Jesus saw Peter, the Rock: "You are Simon son of John. You *will be* called Cephas."[4] In Jesus' eyes, Peter was a fearless evangelist leading a dynamic community of faith where thousands upon thousands of people would be set free. Jesus saw the man who would stand with undaunted courage before the rulers, the elders, and the teachers of the law and boldly proclaim the fulfillment of Scripture. He looked straight into Simon's eyes and spoke words of creation. "From now on you will catch men."[5] A few years down the road, others could hardly believe the transformation: "When they saw the courage of Peter and John and realized that they were unschooled, ordinary men, they were astonished and they took note that these men had been with Jesus."[6]

As the Spirit opens our eyes, the everyday course of our lives becomes an adventure of innovation. Everywhere we look, fields are ripe for harvest. When teachers enter their classrooms, they should enter with confidence, knowing that God is already there, and he is already creating, calling, and arranging his purposes in the individual lives of each student. Teachers who live by faith see their students as works of art in progression toward the people God is creating them to become. For those who live by faith, confrontational and critical people are seen as allies who are helping us to grow stronger. Parents become far more aware of the immense possibilities hidden in their children. Spouses long to see their partners set free to fulfill their dreams. Everything is potential — every person sitting around the table has something of immense value to contribute.

As the Spirit opens your eyes, what will he allow you to see? He will show you greater possibilities than you have ever dreamed before. Recently I traveled to Africa to figure out what it would take to open a new school in an area that, according to UN data, is the poorest on the planet, per capita. While I was there, the temperature soared to 126 degrees Fahrenheit. Many of the roads are so rutted that they can be navigated only with four wheelers. Dust finds its way into everything. Throughout the entire bone-dry region, I saw almost no grass. Even in the countryside there are few gardens. Some children don't know how it feels to take a gulp from a bottle of water. Even the camels foam at the mouth.

Now imagine my surprise when, after I had been there for a few days, my hosts took me across one of the largest rivers in Africa, which flows directly through the city. As I drove over a bridge and looked down into that blue water, I could scarcely believe what I was seeing. With only minimal investment, a bit of expertise, and some initiative, an entire nation could be set free from its parched condition. Images of African children sprinting across green lawns and splashing one another with Super Soakers raced through my imagination. Thousands are a few short steps away from activating a mighty resource that God has already hidden in plain sight, yet day after day they continue plodding through their thirsty existence. They have already been given everything they need to transform their wind-blown dust into a great African bread basket. The one missing ingredient? Faith.

That sparkling river streaming day and night through the dust is a vivid reminder that God's grace abounds "in all things at all times."[7] Our loving Creator has already done for us "immeasurably more than all we ask or imagine."[8] We wake up every morning with the abundance of his grace streaming all around us. Everything we can possibly dream that is healthy, pure, beneficial, and beautiful may be closer than we can imagine. Grace is a mighty river flowing from God's loving heart. It whispers, beckons, calls out, and kisses us. It also growls, swarms, roars, and storms. Grace dares us to open our eyes and dream greater dreams. Dreams that are born in faith and that challenge the impossible. Dreams that defiantly move against strongholds that enslave and suffocate humanity. Dreams that fuel our imaginations and redirect the course of history. Grace dares us to open our eyes and see the river, catching a glimpse of the unlimited possibilities all around us.

Incidentally, God had an even greater surprise waiting for me in West Africa. Would you imagine that leaders in a predominantly Muslim nation would gratefully open their arms to a Christian school? I was told, "The day you open a school like that, you will be educating the future leaders of this country." When I hear statements like that, I realize that all of my life I've been walking blind. God is just beginning to crack open my eyes to the fact that he has no limitations. If I just step forward in response to his voice, he will always make a way. He is showing me that the greatest barriers to his artistry in and through my life are not physical dangers nor are they menacing ogres who believe in other religions. The real barriers are my own conjured fears and the imaginary monsters in my own closet. These fears are phony castle walls I've constructed around me. Can you just imagine me, a grown man, sitting on the shore and believing that my sand castle will protect me? These silly little walls might give me a secure feeling, but one wave from the ocean would annihilate them.

Bono sings it best in U2's "Stand Up Comedy": "Out from under your beds!"[9] May I ask? What are your mental security blankets? A young man asked Jesus what he must do to inherit eternal life. After mentioning obedience to the commandments, Jesus said, "You still lack one thing. Sell everything you have and give to the poor, and you will have treasure in heaven. Then come, follow me."[10] Luke observes that the man went away very sad, because he had great wealth. Here's another way of looking at it: The man had constructed a one-foot-tall sand castle when most of the others around him had three-inch-tall sand castles. Imagine the monsters in the poor man's closet! What if he'd thrown his money to the wind and stepped over the edge like Matthew or Zacchaeus? But no, following Jesus requires faith, and faith is always agonizing. The man's power base would evaporate. His financial safety nets would be torn out from under his feet. How would he pay for his children's college education? Jesus, of course, knew that he was calling a rich man into a much greater kind of wealth. He was calling a man to rise up out of his paltry bank vault, to run toward the horizon and dive into the waves and swim to a freedom more luxurious than his impoverished mind could possibly imagine. Jesus was calling a prisoner to find a life on the edge—a life of constantly unfolding new possibilities. A life reserved only for the few who dare to live by faith.

CHARIOTS OF FIRE

What will it be like for you and me as the Spirit of God walks us farther and farther down the corridor of faith? Our expanding vision will affect every element of our lives. The Spirit will teach us what to say in every conversation. He will show us how to respond to every problem, regardless of how big or small.

In 2 Kings we read that Elisha was in a heap of trouble. The king of Aram was hunting him down and had found out where Elisha was. During the night the king's army had surrounded the city where Elisha was sleeping. When Elisha's servant saw what a pickle they were in, he responded like I probably would. He panicked. But Elisha wasn't fazed. He could see a bit deeper into reality. "Elisha prayed, and said, 'LORD, I pray, open his eyes that he may see.' Then the LORD opened the eyes of the young man, and he saw. And behold, the mountain was full of horses and chariots of fire all around Elisha."[11]

You and I may not be able to see the chariots of fire all around us, but faith assures us that they are there. From the future, God has already hidden in place the solutions to the challenges I will face tomorrow. My ability to improvise requires no more than to open my eyes to a different, more imaginative solution—one that a supremely creative God has put before me, ready and waiting.

Years ago, Cyndi and I were getting a team of five college students ready for a summer mission trip overseas. However, there was a problem. These particular college students and a flight across the Pacific Ocean did not belong in the same sentence, at least financially. They still calculated their financial worth each time they scrounged in their pockets for quarters to do laundry. Luckily, they had enough faith to believe that God would make a way. Our journey required about $2,000 per team member. As the date for departure drew closer, we were still about $8,000 short of what we needed as a team, and this would take a miracle.

For a few Saturdays, we held yard sales. I waved good-bye to several outdated sweaters, some scratchy Charlie Patton and Herb Alpert records, and a dusty nightstand with one cracked leg. Then someone suggested selling roses. One Friday morning we took every dollar that we had saved from yard sales and we went down to the flower market in Los Angeles. We bought hundreds of roses, then scattered to different busy intersections around the city. That night, we regrouped at my house. Our car trunks were still brimming with roses. We had vastly overestimated the desire of men in Los Angeles to buy roses for their significant others. We were in a quandary, the pressure was mounting, and the panic button was beginning to flash. We had to sell seven hundred roses fast. Some were already starting to wilt.

Then we saw the chariots of fire. Well, they weren't exactly chariots, and they weren't exactly on fire. But the answer God gave us had something to do with the Coliseum. We remembered that a large gathering of Christian men was going to take place in the Los Angeles Coliseum the next morning. All day long, they were going to be reminded how much they treasure and cherish their wives. Sure enough, we hit the jackpot. Men were piling onto buses to go back to their distant churches. I picked my first bus, took a deep breath, and climbed on. Standing next to the driver, I announced,

"I've got roses here for you to take home to your wife. She's worth every dollar you'll spend, isn't she? And by the way, every sale goes to support college students who want to take a mission trip to Asia!" Bus after bus, we ended up selling every rose that hadn't wilted or lost its petals.

Later that night, we exulted together in what God had done. Although we felt we had seen a miracle, the solution to our problem had been there all along. God was just waiting for us to *see* it. That experience was the perfect prerequisite for the challenges we would experience on the other side of the planet. Our trip to Asia would be sprinkled with twisting turns, surprising changes in plans, and unexpected illnesses. We would need to huddle together and respond with faith, knowing that God had put into place the answer to each seemingly impossible dilemma.

Like a father hiding Easter eggs in a garden for his children, God surrounds us with pearls of possibility. They can be found in the most unexpected and surprising places. For me nothing demonstrates this more than when I make treks deep into the Borneo jungle. As my shoes slip along mucky trails, my eyes see thorny plants, leeches, thick mud, and vines trying to wrap themselves around me. Because the trees block out the sun, it is easy to become directionally disoriented. But for my Dayak friends who were born out there, the jungle is not so menacing. After centuries of surviving the swamps, they've discovered which plants are useful, which roots they can dig up for food, and what tree trunks hold the tastiest grubs. They know where to find honey and what streams offer the most fish. They know how to trap wild boar. In other words, they see the jungle like I see a grocery store or like my children see a playground. Through the centuries, the Dayaks have uncovered myriad possibilities for survival where a first-time visitor is overwhelmed with fear. I know it's not funny, but I'll write it anyway: It's a jungle out there. But if that's where God calls you, trust him! Listen to his voice, let him open your eyes and transform your regions of fear and helplessness into a playground.

CHASING NEW HORIZONS ∽

The writer of Hebrews defines faith as "the substance of things hoped for, the evidence of things not seen."[12] There's nothing passive about faith. Faith is the catalyst of an activated hope, a confident expectation that our hearts' passion to unearth evidence of the unseen will be fulfilled. Even if our hunger to see more deeply into the vast ocean of possibility has been muted since we've grown up, all of us were born with exploring minds. As small children, we hungered for a deeper understanding of the world around us. We incessantly pelted our parents and teachers with questions. The insatiable curiosity that we observe in small children is a clue to the instinctive hunger for exploration that God plants inside his image bearers. Every child's question reminds us that God created us to be drawn by the power of faith through the ever expanding corridor of truth. He has created us with a ravenous hunger to see, to be pulled into mysterious territory by our own curiosity.

The inside story of the Wright brothers is one of the most heroic adventures in curiosity I've ever heard of. Time after time, Orville and Wilbur were faced with barriers that the engineering world had deemed impossible to cross. The brothers spent countless hours with binoculars studying birds, searching for the secrets of flight. To them, birds in flight were evidence that human flight was also possible. Everything they learned from watching birds, they took back into their workshop. When they realized that all existing engines were too heavy, they invented their own lighter engine. They experimented with hundreds of variations of possible wings and propeller shapes. Slowly and surely, one step led to the next until they rose up into the skies. I wasn't surprised when I read that Orville and Wilbur were committed believers and that their father was a pastor. Their remarkable journey of exploration was launched from the unshakeable belief that with God nothing is impossible.

My own dad's inventiveness doesn't quite match the Wright brothers. But he did invent the world's first digital chess clock. He named it the Kaisha 1000. For a while he marketed it, then he sold the patent. To him, marketing the chess clock was a tedious bore. His real joy was in the process of exploration, figuring out how to do something no one had ever done before. His delight was in discovering a better way to play speed chess. Does it seem, well, odd that a missionary who lived deep in the jungle with a tribe of cannibals would take the time to invent the world's first digital chess clock? Perhaps the two fit quite naturally together in the same person. After all, the prerequisite for both endeavors is faith.

A few months ago, I was seated in a float plane soaring over the jungles of Papua in the direction of the villages where my parents first went in 1962. Looking out of my window, I gazed down on swamps that stretched to the horizon in every direction. We were still a half hour from our destination. Then, suddenly, far below, I noticed a cluster of four thatched-roofed houses carved out of the jungle. What extreme isolation! As I looked down on those thatched roofs, I wondered what they did every day. Even more amazing, *why* would humans travel so far? It would have required months of paddling and trekking to migrate that deep into the swamps.

If you have a globe or a world map, take a look at the remote south Pacific islands like Bora Bora, Vanuatu, and Samoa. Look at how far apart they are. Historians have various theories about how people wound up in places like that. Far more interesting to me is *why* anyone would migrate there. What would cause someone to climb into a canoe and paddle into the open sea in search of a hidden world beyond the horizon? The fact that people launched away from familiar shores at risk of their own lives reveals a deep, vibrant hunger for exploration that their Creator has infused into the human spirit.

Humanity, what a strange, magnificent creation you are! From the day you were formed from the dust and God breathed into your soul, you've had a craving to know what you have never known before. You have migrated across mysterious, uncharted waters. Your hands can be seen endlessly exploring along the necks of your guitars, making friends with new chords, scales, and arpeggios. In school you quietly stare out of your classroom windows at the distant mountains. You trekked into the Andes Mountains and rode Arabian stallions into the Sahara. You migrated from Siberia across the Straits into America. When all the blank canvases on your maps had been charted, you started looking down rather than out. Migrating through microscopes, you explored cells, molecules, atoms, quarks, and leptons. To this day, you are combining, straining, pondering, wondering, and marveling at God's multivalent creation.

As I consider humanity's epic journey of exploration through history, I can also detect an important aspect of God's personality. Why didn't he simply explain to our ancestors how to dig for iron ore, smelt steel, or shape the wing of an aircraft? Why didn't he just show us how to communicate using high-frequency radio waves? He at least could have showed someone the blueprints! But instead God infused into his creation billions and billions of untapped possibilities, then he matched those possibilities by inserting a relentless hunger for exploration in his image bearers.

We are borne on the shoulders of those who moved out into the remaining realms of truth and uncovered pearls of great worth. Men and women of faith aren't just tourists when they look through microscopes. They mine their specimens for value, longing, praying, and searching for a cure to an "incurable" illness. *Perhaps today I will find the answer under these high-powered lenses.* Each time one of God's image bearers discovers another pearl in creation, we come one step closer to the hot, flaming center of truth. Solomon called it wisdom. Wisdom is not somewhere back there. Wisdom is a voice calling in the streets. She speaks with divinely ordained purpose. She walks somewhere out in front of us, only now and then stopping to look back over her shoulder. Her voice calls gently. She lights up our paths as she beckons us to advance forward.

CHASING GOD ∽

God is waiting in all of his glorious beauty at the far end of the corridor. He is the ultimate destination of human curiosity. Jesus promised that those who ask will receive, those who seek will find, and for those who knock a door will be opened.[13] God has always promised that if we search for him, he will reveal himself: "You will seek me and find me when you seek me with all your heart."[14] Moses told the Hebrews in the wilderness that their descendants would wander away from God. They would be scattered to the wind. From various nations across the earth they would even begin worshiping idols. Moses assures them, "But if from there you seek the LORD your God, you will find him if you look for him with all your heart and with all your soul."[15] Over and over, God reveals himself as a Father who delights in those moments when his children respond to his whispered invitation, "Come and find me, treasured ones."

C. S. Lewis could see down the corridor. As an Oxford professor, he had his share of conversations with very smart people who found the courage to seek God with their minds but were too afraid to seek him with their souls. He typed one such conversation into his children's novel *Prince Caspian*, where we find a child named Lucy (That's our girl!) and her brother Edmund peering into the corridor.

> "There. There. Don't you see? Just this side of the trees."
>
> Edmund stared hard for a while and then said, "No. There's nothing there. You've got dazzled and muddled with the moonlight. One does, you know. I thought I saw something for a moment myself. It's only an optical what-do-you-call-it."
>
> "I can see him all the time," said Lucy. "He's looking straight at us."
>
> "Then why can't I see him?"

"He said you mightn't be able to."

"Why?"

"I don't know. That's just what he said."

"Oh, bother it all," said Edmund. "I do wish you wouldn't keep on seeing things."[16]

Be assured that if your heart and soul seek after God, you will "keep on seeing things." You won't just catch a glimpse of God in the trees. You will begin to see him everywhere. You won't just hear his voice on the occasional Sunday morning. You will begin to hear him whispering, guiding, calling, and moving all around you. You will begin to grasp what it means to pray without ceasing.

Last night Cyndi and I were at a birthday dinner. I found myself sitting across from a lady named Amy. Amy grew up in Pennsylvania. After hearing that she was raised by a nonpracticing Catholic father and an atheist mother, I asked her, "Tell me, when you were a little girl growing up in that environment, did your soul ever cry out for God?"

Amy's eyes immediately welled up with tears. "More than you might ever imagine." Is Amy's answer the rare exception? Are the majority of people around us rather more like unseeing Edmund than divergent-minded Lucy? No, Lucy's is by far the normal human experience. All across the earth, humanity hungers to know the One who made them. God is opening eyes and responding to the hearts of his children. Jesus said, "Blessed are the pure in heart, for they will see God."[17] This blessing reminds me of my friend Juliana. A few years ago, a group of us fulfilled a dream we'd talked about for several years: to launch a magazine for educators across Indonesia. Today, hundreds of teachers wait eagerly for each new edition. Juliana is the editor. She was raised a Muslim, and her heart's tale of being drawn into God's radiant light reminds me that people we meet every day are hungering for God more than we imagine.

Juliana lived in the slums of a city called Bandung. She was ten years old when an American couple named Steve and Claire moved in next door. Nearly every afternoon on her way home from school Juliana waited by her gate until she could get another look at them.

Steve and Claire were different from anyone Juliana had ever known. They were so warm and friendly. She waited as long as three hours just to catch a glimpse of their radiant faces. She remembers thinking, *Why are they living here? Surely they were rich enough to live in a bigger house than that!* Steve and Claire often took walks together in the late afternoons. They were always smiling and laughing from the heart as they stumbled through their new Indonesian words with their neighbors or kicked a rattan ball around with the boys in the alley.

One day Steve and Claire invited Juliana into their house. She came in cautiously. There she saw a cross on their bookshelf, and she saw Claire reading a Bible. Being from a Muslim family, Juliana had been told many times that she should stay away from crosses and Bibles. She started to feel nervous. But she was drawn to the mysterious peacefulness in that house. She couldn't explain it. Whatever it was, she had never felt it before, and she suspected it had something to do with Jesus. He was the one they were so often talking about. Yes, it had to be Jesus who was calling out to her from Steve and Claire's house. One day Claire offered Juliana a Bible. But she refused to accept it. She knew it would bring nothing but trouble into her life.

After only a few months, Steve and Claire moved away, but the words they had planted and the peace that flowed from their home were gripping and beautiful to Juliana's heart. She desperately wanted to find out more about this Jesus.

By the time Juliana graduated from grade six, she could stand it no longer. She could not get her wonderment about this Jesus out of her mind. Juliana knew that she might find out more about Jesus if she transferred to a Christian junior high school. She began pleading with her parents to let her transfer to a Christian school. They refused, but Juliana was stubborn. She pressed on until they finally relented, but they told her not even to think about visiting a church. Juliana's parents were nervous about the religion, but they knew that their daughter would receive a much more effective education at the Christian school.

At her new school, Juliana started reading a Bible. She began to blossom into a new way of life consumed with love for Jesus and for other people. When Juliana was twelve, she was baptized— to the horror and dismay of her parents. They had sternly warned her to stay away from church, but she was very stubborn. Every Sunday, she tried to find new ways to slip out of the house and run off to church, even though it meant that she would receive a severe beating when she came home.

When Juliana's grandmother found out that she had started going to church, she stopped talking to her. Every day Juliana came into her grandmother's room and cried and tried to hug her. But her grandmother just looked the other way. She did not say even one word to Juliana, though Juliana never stopped visiting her. Week after week, month after month, their conversation was a one way street. Little did Juliana know at the time that, day after day, she was planting and watering seeds of life in her family's hearts. Eventually Juliana moved away from home, and her love for her family grew and matured. Juliana persistently came to see her grandmother every day after school.

One day when Juliana was nineteen years old, she came down with the flu. She was too sick to go back home for her daily visit. Suddenly the phone rang. It was her grandmother's voice on the line, wondering why she had not come. It was the first time her grandmother had spoken directly to Juliana in seven years. That phone call was the breakthrough moment. Steve and Claire had planted seeds of life in Juliana's soul that had multiplied and were just beginning to burst out and bear fruit in the other members of her family. When Juliana was twenty-one, her mother believed and was baptized. Her little brother became a believer, and eventually her father also believed and was baptized when Juliana was twenty-two.

Jesus said that from the cross he would *draw* all of humanity to himself.[18] This word, according to Vine's Concordance, refers to a movement from within by inward power.[19] Juliana's narrative is a reminder that our Creator has planted an insatiable curiosity in our souls so that we will search for him and find him. Jesus also promised his disciples that the Spirit would guide them into *all* truth.[20] I can't imagine what "all truth" might really mean *yet*, but I can be sure of two things. First, Jesus saw vastly more than others around him were able to see. Speaking to people whose eyes were perfectly functional, Jesus told them they were actually blind.[21] Second, by walking in his Spirit, I position myself to see more than I've ever seen before.

Your life, right now, is brimming with limitless opportunities to bring hope into the waiting world. You can take any gift that

God has infused into your life and stretch it into eternal dimensions. To invest a talent, a spiritual gift, a skill set, a wallet full of cash, or anything else that God has placed under your control on behalf of others honors and glorifies your Creator. It's a chance to declare the greatness of your God by dreaming, chasing, and activating the possibilities he has already planted within you and around you.

The time has come for Spirit-fueled entrepreneurs, inventors, and explorers to step to the forefront of the kingdom of God and make our voices heard. We have entered our century of opportunity. The Creator of the universe has led the nations to this moment in history. The planet's most desperate caverns of darkness are like blank canvases calling out to be painted. The souls around you are hungering for God. People are eager and ready to listen. All of the medicines that can heal all the diseases in the entire world are already here and have always been here. The cures to HIV/AIDS, cancer, cystic fibrosis, and autism are so, *so* close. God has already set into place all of the answers to all of the broken and fallen conditions of the universe — even our own fallen selves. The only thing that stands in your way is fear. Open your eyes to God's vision. Listen for his voice. Approach the edge and take a breath. Anticipate.

CHAPTER 7

RELEASE

SCALING MOUNTAINS

Sadly, all honeymoons must end. But, happily for us, at the end of our honeymoon a pile of wedding presents awaited. Cyndi and I arrived home from Los Cabos to find our living room floor hidden beneath a mountain of gifts. With a duet of *oohs* and *aahs*, we tore open a pile of coffee mugs, can openers, bathroom towels, and other goodies. But the best wedding gift I opened that day was the last one. My bride took me by the hand and led me out into the driveway, where I looked into the dashboard of my convertible VW Cabriolet—and noticed a German-made Blaupunkt stereo she'd had installed while we were away. Instantly that stereo became my most prized possession. My heart valued it even more than the car it had been installed in.

One morning I strolled out to my snazzy little car, swinging my keys and whistling, only to discover that the driver's window was scattered in a million little pieces. Then I noticed a jagged wound in my dashboard. I had been Blaupunkted! If you've ever

been robbed, you can relate to the shocked and wounded disbelief I felt in that moment. For weeks I remained heartsick every
time I climbed into my car. We weren't able to afford another
stereo like it, and what could replace the sentimental value of a
wedding present from my own wife? Each morning and afternoon I tried not to look at the gaping hole in front of me. Silence
was salt in my wound. I was being forced to head into my day
without my soul coffee. As I waited at traffic lights, music drifting
from other cars was so irritating.

Then something unexpected began to happen in my heart.
Extended silence opened a portal of communication with God.
After a few weeks of driving in the fumes of my irritation, the
Spirit gracefully began to whisper into my silence. We started to
have conversations. I'd pray about the matters that weighed heavy
on my heart, and he'd answer. He'd put the faces of certain people
into my mind and nudge my heart to pray for them. Together,
we'd think through the coming appointments and issues of the
day and God would give me insights on how to approach them.
Each morning, my ability to listen increased. In a way that I'd
never previously experienced, God's passions and priorities began
to take precedence over my own. Before long, I began to look
forward to these conversations so much that I was grateful for the
silence. Having been torn away from something I had treasured
so deeply, I found myself beginning to understand what it means
to live in a growing, thriving relationship with God.

Eventually, though, the Spirit decided to test my ability to
listen in the midst of some pressure. One afternoon I found my
Blaupunkt. It had been installed in the dashboard of my friend's
truck. Now this wasn't just some Blaupunkt—it was actually
mine. And it wasn't just some guy I had met once or twice—he

was an old friend from church. I said, "Hey, that's funny. That looks like my stereo." Turns out he'd just bought it off of a gangster who lived right around the corner from my house.

I doubt I've ever been so angry. My own friend would knowingly buy my stereo from a thief and keep it for himself? Wow, I guess it was "finders keepers." *Who does he think I am?* Momentarily speechless, I took a deep breath and got ready to erupt in anger. Just then, in the momentary calm before the storm, the Spirit whispered a word into my heart.

Release!

I exhaled quietly, released the prized possession, then simply went on living. That was a breakthrough moment in my life. Hearing God's command then responding as he instructed me to respond was exhilarating. The freedom I felt in the aftermath of that moment left me humming a new song.

God's voice always moves us in the direction of freedom. His dreams carry us toward spaces so wide that our minds cannot possibly imagine. If we could only see the people he is calling us to become, we would wonder if it were even possible to change that much! God wants to open our eyes to see unimaginable beauty, a wondrous beauty that brings us to our knees. He wants to lift and carry us into the wind and over the waves. We are designed—with all of our lightning-fast reflexes and highly tuned senses and uncanny intuition—to exude hope even in the face of life's menacing reversals of fortune. We are designed to plunge into roaring rapids, to scramble up mountains, and to storm fortresses. We are custom-built to rise to a challenge, to guide a ship through a storm, to take authority over demons. We are made to stop working for a few moments to pray for the person at the office who has just expressed frustration at her failed marriage.

The outer layers of our lives churn with conflicting schedules, illegible shopping lists, endless lines at the bank, mid-afternoon soccer practice, and marathon staff meetings. Yet beneath it all, the Spirit of God beckons our souls to breathe in elegant simplicity. Even on pressure-filled days, we must be free to pick up the pace or slow down. Free to stop and worship God for a few minutes. Free to weep openly when we experience grief. Free to laugh from the soul. Free to lift our hands to heaven and worship God without fear of what others might think. Free to openly confess our sins. Free to listen to the hearts and dreams of those around us. As a husband and father, God calls me to be able to look at Cyndi and Katie and whisper to them, "You are so beautiful." He calls me to be a father who looks over my sons' homework and says, "Stephen and Josiah, you make me so proud!" The Spirit calls us to be so radically liberated that, in any given moment, we can pray for a complete stranger while standing in line at the hardware store. He draws us toward a miraculous freedom, the unhindered ability to respond from our hearts, "I am so sorry!" or "Will you forgive me?" Or maybe even, "I see that your idea is much better than mine—let's go with your way." To taste of this freedom, we must make a life habit of letting go. Along the winding, fluctuating paths into the future, we must be quick to say, "Release!"

So far in this book, we have delved into what it means to listen for the Spirit's voice. We've been called to move out in response to God's love for the world around us. We considered how faith opens our vision to see the world through God's eyes. We honed in on the way God is already out there in the realm of the unknown, preparing our circumstances for our leaps of faith. We also touched on the hunger to explore that God infuses in our souls, and identified this hunger as one of God's chosen catalysts of response. Even now, as you are nearing the end of this book, perhaps there is still a reluctance to live your faith at the edge.

What stands in your way?

My own heart has a tendency to clutch physical, emotional, and mental objects and lug them around with me. As a result, my freedom to live in the Spirit gets tangled up. Can you relate? Could it be that our greatest barriers to freedom are our own heart addictions—the synthetic elements that substitute God? Our possessions, heart addictions, and our compulsive needs can enslave us—or they can be released forever, setting us free to truly live in the freedom of the Spirit. With each turn of a page, ask God to show you anything that hinders your response to his voice. Remember that the end game of this chapter is your own freedom.

FATHER-DAUGHTER DATE ∽

Remember what it was like to be a small child? Does your soul contain any remnants of those days when the world was a playground and you were free to catch tadpoles and chase butterflies across a field? My daughter helps me remember what it was like to live in the freedom of faith. Katie's eyes are filled with dreams. She lives to serve the poor, the disenfranchised, and the victims of disasters. She has journeyed with Cyndi and me to various islands and countries to serve children in Mustard Seed International's orphanages and schools. Katie likes to keep an open suitcase in her room where she puts anything she can find that might be able to help other children in need. When she was nine, an earthquake devastated a cluster of villages and towns just a few hours' drive from where we were living. Over 100,000 homes were shaken into piles of rubble, and thousands died in the wreckage. The people of that area were suffering under the strain of a double dose of terror. A volcano near them was threatening to unleash a flow of molten lava into their rice paddies and darken their skies with volcanic ash.

Within days I was meeting with leaders from two other organizations to formulate a response. Our immediate strategy was to help a thousand families. This would involve sending out an urgent plea to donors, followed by purchasing and carrying tons of rice, tents, blankets, cooking supplies, vegetables, and generators into the disaster zone. Meanwhile, as I was on the phone making arrangements, Katie was quietly listening. When she heard me say that I would be making a trip into the destruction zone, she made sure I knew that she would be coming along.

When our team pulled into the earthquake-ravaged area, Katie couldn't wait to jump off the bus. She immediately walked into the village and gathered children who had slept under the stars for three weeks. I had explained to her that many of these kids were suffering from something called post-traumatic stress. She helped organize an art contest. She handed out colored pens and paper, and asked the other children to draw pictures.

On the second day, she was on her own in another village. By the time she left, dozens of kids were singing, "Selamat jalan dan terima kasih, Katie!" *Farewell and thank you, Katie!* I couldn't help but notice that Katie's heart was filled with compassion and equally bursting out with joy at the chance to serve others. On the third day, we sifted through the rubble of a man's home, separating the salvageable bricks and roof tiles from the broken pieces. She worked tirelessly and joyfully in the hot, equatorial sun. Later that afternoon, our team gathered over a hundred children for a program of soccer, games, music, and a drama. Katie was up front helping to lead the songs.

As we all climbed onto the bus to come home after the fourth day, Katie plopped down in the seat next to me and melted into my left arm. She was played out. I wrapped her up and kissed her on the forehead. My own heart was bursting with delight at having experienced four days of working from sunrise to late at night alongside my own daughter. Her fullness of heart makes this father proud.

More than once I've heard screaming coming from Katie's room. I've rushed in there, wondering if she's been hurt, only to discover that all that noise is just her response to a surprising twist in the plot of an *American Girl* novel. Katie can't keep still or quiet while watching a movie, especially if it has any romance whatsoever. To sit next to her in a theater is to hear two hours' worth of sighing.

Katie's way of living reminds me of Paul's words in Colossians: "Whatever you do, work at it with all your heart, as working for the Lord."[1] For me, though, the quest to live in such a way sometimes feels beyond reach. I want to rise up into each day and go to sleep every night having lived with a full heart, but long ago I discovered that full hearts are the ones that get wounded and broken. I wonder how my daughter will handle it if or when someday her heart gets trampled. Will she close herself off from those pure, streaming, and free-spirited emotions of life? I pray that nothing will ever tear that unreserved passion away from her soul.

As I look back at my own life, I wonder if it's even possible to grow up in this world without one's heart getting shredded now and then. In response to our most forgettable heartaches, many

of us have closed ourselves off, locked our hearts behind unassailable walls, and hidden away the key. Then our emotions, which
God entrusted to us to be expressed purely, freely, and heartily,
begin to drift, blown like a ship with a broken mast in the open
sea. Eventually, some drift for so many years that we can't even
imagine what it would feel like to live with reckless abandon-
ment for God.

THE SPINNING MAN ∽

When I was a boy growing up in California, my neighborhood
seemed to hold a quixotic allure for those who had yanked their
mental anchors out of reality and decided to drift in a dreamy
world. One fellow grabbed my sleeve just outside the local donut
shop. "See this gold watch? I can throw it all the way around
the *wooorld!*" Then he screamed, angrily wrestled the watch off
his wrist with a burst of triumph over his bondage to time, and
hurled it. Unfortunately, my forehead got in the way of the flight
path. He apologized when he saw me wiping the blood from
my brow. Our school cafeteria lady was apparently married to
Muhammad Ali. Sometimes these types would wander into our
church, calling themselves prophets and interrupting our pastor's
sermons by suddenly leaping up from their pews and pronounc-
ing loud strings of nonsensical words about the end times and
God's judgment.

Out of all of these assorted characters, one rose above the
crowd to become our favorite superhero of irrelevance. My
friends and I were in awe of this man. Affectionately known as
the Spinning Man, he had already spun himself into an urban
legend by the time I entered high school. While other citizens

went about their daily activities, working, building, and shopping, the Spinning Man would spin. We occasionally spotted him in unexpected corners of our town, twirling like a ballerina for hour after hour, day after day, year after year. Just the thought of him still makes me dizzy. I confess that on a hot afternoon, I lobbed a water balloon at the Spinning Man. My aim was true. I watched long enough to notice that even after his baptism, he kept right on spinning. He was so locked away in his own whirling microreality that everyone else had completely disappeared.

I wonder what the Spinning Man was attempting to spin away from. Perhaps he was trying to blur out the misery of an irreparable mistake, the echoes of a ruptured marriage, or the unrelenting sense of personal failure. Most likely, he was simply spinning away from himself.

I know a little bit about that. I know what it is like to lose my heart — and so lose everyone else along the way. My wandering, spinning journey away from my heart originated on my paper route when I was in sixth grade. Seven days a week I would fold up a stack of newspapers, tuck them into a canvas bag, strap them over the handlebars of my bike and spend a few hours delivering them. It was on Sinaloa Street that my childhood came to a screeching halt. There, a man named Phillip waved at me with a warm smile each day. Eventually Phillip and I became friends. I was too young to read the signs. I couldn't have known that he was a chronically sick predator.

For me, the greatest tragedy is not that I endured several months of being strangely manipulated and woven into a web of lies. It is the shadowy years of living with an isolated soul that followed. Anyone else who has been sexually abused or molested might be able to relate to what I went through. Torn apart by

thundering waves of nightmarish guilt, I blamed myself merci-
lessly, to the extent that I could hardly sleep at night. At fourteen,
I would get out of bed, slip out the front door of our house, and
roam the streets in the dark, hating myself and wondering how
God felt about me. Believing that anyone who found out would
immediately reject me, I became a master of double identities.

For years, I lived with this scarlet letter burning in my chest.
And, like a cancer, my secret morphed and multiplied. By the
time I graduated from high school, I lived with the daily awareness that I was like two people. One was the real me, the broken
and scarred soul. My second identity was my mask. He was the
happy guy that everyone else thought they knew. He was the
fairly secure athlete who was a captain on the football team and
faithfully attended church.

VIRTUAL REALITY 〜

I know I'm not the only one who has existed with the dread of
being seen. Of course, I don't just mean our bodies. It's our souls
that must be brought out into full view. It's rather cold out there
in the open, and, through the years, some of us figure out that
by adding on new layers of false identity, our souls can avoid the
chilling stares of others. The problem with these layers is that they
are so monstrously heavy. For whatever reason, we spend so much
time building these layers that we finally decide it's easier just to
hunker down in them. Through the years we haul them around,
bearing their weight until we lose track of who we really are.
Then, like actors who forget that the stage lights have been turned
off and the cameras are no longer rolling, we actually start believing in our own myths.

Gene Simmons of the rock band KISS got away with wearing his black and white costume and facial makeup on stage. But it's unlikely he'd dress like that to fetch a cappuccino and bagel at the corner deli. I can imagine Mel Gibson wearing his Scottish kilt and sword on the set of the film *Braveheart*, yet I doubt he'd pretend to be William Wallace at his daughter's piano recital. So many of us take our acting careers on the road. We travel through our days as if every night were Halloween.

Several years ago I decided to read some of the philosophers who have influenced western civilization. I eagerly dug into Plato, Thomas Aquinas, René Descartes, G. W. F. Hegel, and David Hume. Page after page, these writers gave me a lot to think about, yet I learned almost nothing about the men behind the words. From their writings, we can't divine much about their personalities or how their theories related to the human struggle. They are able to impart vast swatches of transcendent knowledge while holding back their deepest and most personal anxieties. They seem to have a hard time revealing whether they've ever had their hearts broken, experienced difficulties with their marriages, or have ever gone to sleep wishing they would never wake up. For some reason, most philosophy tries to remain aloof from broken hearts and embattled dreams.

Finally, after months of drowning myself in transcendence while ignoring the personal implications, I picked up the poetry of David. Here, in the Psalms, was a breath of fresh air. David knew what it means to stagger under the weight of another man's armor, and he wanted none of that. Instead, David preferred a more buoyant and agile way of life. David and the other psalmists wrote out of the rapid, swirling intersections between God, paradox, mystery, and the human soul. They personally and intimately grappled with humanity's struggle for meaning and existence. When David sat down to write, he wasn't worried about what others would think or whether he'd be liked. He wasn't concerned with his reputation. His poetry was as gritty, raw, and real as life itself. He poured himself out, freely and openly expressing his weaknesses, confusion, doubts, pain, and even hatred. Sentences like, "I am weary with my crying; My throat is dry; My eyes fail while I wait for my God,"[2] define his writing style.

The freedom in David's poetry reminds me of the apostle Paul. Though Paul did not write poetry, he still expresses the same depth of passion. He writes from the heart: "For out of much affliction and anguish of heart I wrote to you, with many tears, not that you should be grieved, but that you might know the love which I have so abundantly for you."[3] In another place he writes, "I came to you in weakness and fear, and with much trembling. My message and my preaching were not with wise and persuasive words, but with a demonstration of the Spirit's power, so that your faith might not rest on men's wisdom, but on God's power."[4] Paul's way of living and loving with such a full heart was contagious. When he said good-bye to the leaders of the church in Ephesus for the last time, they responded by weeping as they embraced him and kissed him.[5] Paul had served them with a full and unreserved heart, holding nothing back.

The writings of David and Paul help us to understand the depth and honesty which foster a thriving relationship with God. Our relationships with one another also erupt with life when we find one another's souls. Some call this way of life "being transparent." Others refer to it as showing one's true colors. I call it veracity — a way of life that is continually stripping off the enslaving masks that weigh down our souls, and journeying with God in the freedom of truth, even if that truth sometimes hurts.

CRACKING THE SECRET CODE ∽

Argentine born and raised, Carlos Tévez is one of the great soccer players alive today. He is a masterful passer and seemingly effortless scorer. If you ever get the chance to watch him take the pitch, you won't be able to ignore his lightning speed. One other thing, though, is immediately noticeable about this man. He has a scar that begins on his cheek and runs all the way down his neck onto his chest. When Tévez was two years old, a kettle of boiling water fell over him, leaving him with such severe burns that he almost lost his life and was forced to spend two months strapped to a hospital bed.

When Carlos became a professional player, his first team offered to pay for him to get plastic surgery. But he would have none of it, saying that the scar was an inseparable part of his life story. He would rather live with his scarred neck freely exposed to the world. That level of freedom inspires me. Everything in my life is a part of who I am. Even my failures and mistakes are tiles in the mosaic that is me. I want to live in the light. I want to bring all of my life freely before my God and the world around me, whether others find me pleasant to look at or not.

We in the Christian world can take a lesson from Carlos Tévez. The shelves of our bookstores today are loaded with insightful books on subjects like spiritual growth, parenting, and marriage. They lay down seven steps to intimacy or ten ways to have a better prayer life. Yet perhaps we need a little more reading material that reaches for the heart and exposes the true conditions within us. Perhaps we are thirsty for works of art that are created by men and women who have grappled with failure and desperation and are not afraid to admit it.

Vipers' Tangle by François Mauriac is a novel about an immensely wealthy man named Louis, whose wife and grown children lazily hang around the mansion, anxiously waiting for the day they can collect their inheritance and be rid of him. Louis sits alone in his room, and begins to write a letter to his wife, Isa, recounting their decades of painful marriage. Not long after their wedding, he had discovered that she still carried lingering memories of a former lover. Torn apart by his wounded heart and her stubborn, petty unwillingness to forgive his tantrums, they were never able to reconcile. They ended up living estranged from one another under the same roof for half a century.

Early in his letter, Louis is bent on pouring out his long-held hatred against his wife. Deeply wounded and steeped in decades of bitterness, he passionately, even viciously writes of how it feels to have his only chance at love torn from his grasp. Then the old man awakens into a painful awareness of his own inner darkness. The real story is the story of his own heart, and Louis finds himself in a conversation with God. The plot crests with his desperate cry for forgiveness, as Louis tears the heavy layers off of his soul, "I know this heart of mine," he says, "this heart; this tangle of vipers. Stifled under them, steeped in their venom, it goes on beating under the swarming of them: this tangle of vipers that is impossible to separate, that needs to be cut loose with the slash of a knife, with the stroke of a sword."[6]

Only a writer who has tangled with his own vipers could write a book so richly filled with understanding of the human experience. A Frenchman who won the Nobel Prize for literature, Mauriac reaches through time and exposes us to the arrogance and selfishness concealed in our own souls. His art confronts us while also daring us to take a leap of faith, to make a dash for our internal prison walls and jump for freedom—the freedom of transparency.

Reading Mauriac can feel like taking a cold shower early in the morning. Great communicators, whether they are writers, filmmakers, parents, teachers, or pastors, are able to masterfully challenge us to deal with our own tangle of vipers. When we put great books back on the shelf or walk out of church, a change has taken place within us. Our secrets have been confronted and exposed. We have wrestled with our own need for God. We have been challenged to take a step of faith, to reach out for our Creator and open our souls to his life-giving Spirit.

What about you and me? We may not aspire to write the next great novel, but we have a choice to live and relate to others with depth, to courageously introduce one another to the agonizing questions and areas of weakness that we face. We can go deeper in our relationships. Perhaps deeper friendships and healthier marriages simply require us to take a good, hard look in the mirror. I've kept a journal with me since I was in college, but it was only a few years ago that I began to write in response to my own internal condition. Each morning in my city, the Islamic call to prayer gets me out of bed around four o'clock. On one of these mornings, I had been restlessly lying awake in the night, stressed out about a strained friendship. After getting out of bed to read my Bible and pray, I decided it was time to get reacquainted with myself. Morning after morning, I continued waking up in the darkness, getting on my knees before God, opening my Bible, then hammering away on the keys of my laptop. I found myself writing tirelessly, expressing my thoughts and feelings.

The following day, I opened up my laptop again and looked at what I had written. In those more reflective moments, I became the objective observer of my own inner world, as if I could see into my own soul. It was almost as if I allowed myself to become another person, then gave that person the right to take a flashlight and look around inside of me. There, in my own words, I caught hints of my deepest secrets. I examined the fears, confusion, pretension, and arrogant attitudes that I had long before hidden away.

I also glimpsed the occasional seeds of eternity that God had quietly hidden within my heart. Sometimes what I found scared me to death. I was surprised to see how cynical and judgmental I really was. False thinking patterns were clustered around my beliefs about God. I unearthed unfair, negative attitudes toward other people. Jesus said that it is what comes out of us that makes us unclean. I began the practice of pressing my finger down on the backspace key, erasing sentences that had been created around lies. Then I typed forward again, filling the void in with truth. Writing in the light was one of the most freeing experiences I've ever had.

WEIGHT TRAINING ∽

So little has been done in Indonesia to influence teenagers for Christ, but God is raising up some amazing people to seek out the lost. One of my passions is to come alongside Indonesian men and women who want to reach out to teenagers. God has given me the chance to meet some inspiring heroes. My friend

Daniel launched a youth church. Through concerts and other outreaches, he has seen more than four hundred kids give their lives to Christ. Timothy is an Indonesian believer who put a successful career as a salesman on hold in order to open a youth center. Today his dream is alive and changing our city. We dream together of someday building a Christian campground where Indonesian youth can come up to the mountains for recreation, outbound adventure, and life-changing appointments with God.

Timothy's youth center hosts a mentoring program every Friday night. Seekers are invited to spend three months with us. The kids are from the eleven different high schools around our city. After some refreshments, music, and activities, we sit down and talk about life. We learn about creativity, and we dream for the future. We highlight character qualities that we desire to embrace. We hone in on our own uniqueness, exploring how God has created us and discovering what it means to be created in the Creator's image. We discuss our responses to the challenges we are facing. We talk about creating the future rather than letting the world create us. We talk about the Messiah, and about love and relationships.

On the first and last weekend of each program, we go camping together. On one of these trips, we took a group of kids to trek 12,060 foot Mount Semeru, one of the tallest volcanoes in Southeast Asia. The hikers were given a list of what they were allowed to put in their backpacks and also what they may not take. Every pack needed to contain only the essentials for the struggle through the clouds toward the frigid summit.

On one particular trek up Mount Semeru, my job was to remain at the back and make sure that the group stayed together. One boy was falling farther and farther behind. He was sweating and struggling, gasping for air, plodding slower and slower. The rest of the group was way ahead and out of sight. Finally I said, "Here, let me carry your pack for you." He gladly unbuckled his pack and let it crash heavily to the ground. When I reached down to pick it up, I could hardly lift it. "What on earth do you have in here?" I opened up his bag and found a radio, a heavy pair of extra shoes that he wouldn't need, more clothes than were on the list, a half a dozen cans of food wrapped up in a pillow case, a video game with cartridges, and a large hunting knife. I took everything that he should never have packed anyway and left it on the side of the trail. This was far too demanding a climb for such foolishness.

Hebrews 12:1 exhorts us to "throw off everything that hinders and the sin that so easily entangles, and let us run with perseverance the race marked out for us." Granted, some of the burdens of life are unavoidable. Yet isn't it obvious that many of us are also being weighed down by frivolous burdens as we plod wearily through our frenzied days? The very items that we imagined would bring freedom have become the extra weights in our backpacks. We are hauling around so much baggage, both internally and externally, that we are not even catching a glimpse of our potential to move in response to God's dreams.

When I was growing up, my dad was a writer, and he was very particular about the words my brothers Steve and Shannon, my sister, Valerie, and I used around the house. The single most despised word on his list was *stuff*. If we used fuzzy words like *stuff*, we were sure to be exhorted to crack them open, revealing the essential substance within. As a result, I've veered away from using *that* word most of my life. But I still need a word to describe the preponderance of, well, *stuff* that clutters up my life. Lately I've chosen *impedimenta*, a word used by the military. When soldiers march for long distances, they must be as light as possible. Any object that is not absolutely necessary for combat readiness is referred to as impedimenta. We, too, must identify the impedimenta in our lives and surrender all that stuff to God. For some the Spirit simply says, "Release what you hold in your hands." For others heart surgery may be required. The Spirit may need to uproot and tear away addictions that have planted themselves deep within us. This uprooting process might even cause severe pain.

Jesus alerts us, "Watch out! ... A man's *life* does not consist in the abundance of his possessions."[7] Perhaps it's time to have a yard sale. Yard sales are interesting places to observe the early stages of freedom. At every yard sale there is a prisoner of impedimenta, posting cardboard signs and begging his neighbors to free him from years of ornamental bondage. Yard sale signs say, "I want to be free! Come, park your car. Wander over here with your hands in your pockets. Please, take my little porcelain swan. Transfer my clutter into your life. Give me a nickel and load up your *own* kitchen with my zillions of bad shopping decisions."

FLOAT LIKE A BUTTERFLY ⌒

Back during the years I worked in Compton, my students would proudly show off the scars from their bullet wounds. One boy lived with a .22 caliber bullet under the skin of his wrist. Sometimes surgeons decide that digging for ammunition will cause more damage than simply leaving it untouched. Do you ever feel like you've got bullets inside of you still? The older we all get, the more scars we have to show. The human heart seems to attract shrapnel.

Sometimes a bullet strikes us from the most unexpected direction. Even the people we love can suddenly and unexpectedly turn against us. I've been struck directly in the heart several times, but one hurt more than all the others. The incident that got me all mixed up happened when I was still working at the international school. Let's call my friend Jack. I had poured a lot of time, energy, and prayer into serving Jack. His first attack came in the highly stressful days following September 11, 2001, when westerners living in Islamic nations were getting jittery. One day Jack came into my office, closed the door, and shouted at me for about two hours. I sat there, speechless. I was being torn up by friendly fire. The force of his anger pressed me back into my chair. I had no idea what to say. Every few minutes I mumbled something in response, but I was too stunned to get much out. Most of the things he was angry about were so easily resolvable.

If that were the end of it, we could have found a quick way out. An apology the next day, something like, "I'm sorry, Paul—I'm just not sure what got into me. I've been under a lot of stress lately." But that shout-down turned out to be only the beginning. In the months following that dark afternoon, Jack ventured into an obsessive quest to derail me from my role as a leader. Whenever I was away, he accused me of one thing or another. Through the months I kept getting hit by sniper bullets. About once a week another false rumor about me would demand my attention.

I was devastated. I didn't know the principles of active engagement. I didn't know that I should've turned *toward* the storm. I should have squarely faced the situation, relentlessly pressing to meet with a third party present until truth broke through and set us both free. If only I would have set aside my pride and fears. If only ...

Instead I retreated into a quiet, seething bitterness.

For me, this betrayal grew like a cancer in my soul. It ballooned into obsessive proportions. My bitterness gained weight daily, expanding into a level of anger that would repeatedly wake me up in the night. I would get up out of bed at 2:00 a.m. and begin swinging my fists into the darkness. Bitterness sucked away my energy. One of my eyes began to twitch. I began to believe that Jack was my archenemy. This monstrously heavy, almost unbearable burden began to wear me down. I felt like I couldn't move.

Everyone around me was affected, and I trusted no one. Cyndi would plead with me to go and talk with him. She tried to find every possible angle to convince me to forgive. But I was powerless to forgive. My bitterness had become my master. I was addicted. My heart was bound and gagged. I had been reduced to a pathetic slave to bitterness. I searched for allies. In casual conversations, I unloaded my pain. I felt I needed a shoulder to complain on. Instead, I was shown little compassion. One guy was amazed that I was taking it all so hard. "Come on, dude. Welcome to the world of leadership, man! We all get nailed. It comes with the job!"

Even after two years, a cloud of anger still hung in the air. But one day, I was standing near my old friend Jack at a soccer game. Speaking for the first time in what must have been over a year, we quickly began yelling, the kind of yelling in which the volume is turned way down but the anger is sky-high. It's the kind of yelling through clenched teeth that married couples sometimes engage in when they don't want to wake up the kids.

Then a miracle happened. That oft-repeated word from the Spirit of God whispered gently in my heart. *Release.* I actually looked my old friend in the eyes and I said, "I'm sorry." But then a second miracle happened. He began apologizing profusely. He begged me for forgiveness. We ended up hugging right there in front of a crowd of people, many of whom had been deeply affected by our little war. I floated home that afternoon. To this day I've been set free from the tonnage of bitterness.

THE LAW THAT GIVES FREEDOM ∽

That experience helped me understand that the three greatest words of release ever spoken were by a man who was bruised, beaten, bleeding, and hanging on a cross. In all of his pain and devastation, he looked down on his betrayers, his murderers, and his tormentors. After one final spray of spit was torpedoed into his face, he lifted his eyes to heaven and unleashed the words that prove to anyone like me that he is indeed the Son of the Living God: "Father, forgive them!"[8]

Jesus was once asked, "Lord, how many times shall I forgive my brother when he sins against me? Up to seven times?"[9] No other person understood forgiveness like Jesus. His method was simple yet brilliant. Forgiveness is a formidable pursuit, like climbing Mount Everest or running a marathon. For Jesus, Peter's question might have sounded something like this, "Lord, how do I get myself ready to finish a marathon?" Cyndi once ran the Los Angeles Marathon. She trained for months. Marathoners begin by running short distances, slowly increasing their regimen. Cyndi was relentless. The key was her daily habit of running. I am convinced that this is what Jesus was talking about when he said, "I tell you, not seven times, but seventy-seven times."[10]

Forgiveness is a discipline of release. It is like a muscle that must be stretched and used repeatedly. The forgiveness muscle is toned and developed in multiple responses to the more petty grievances. It gets a workout in the morning when you see that your husband forgot to put the lid back on the toothpaste tube. Well, that's easy. *I forgive.* Then he forgets to call when he said he would. That one is a little bit tougher. *It hurts, but I will forgive.* That night he is fifteen minutes late for dinner. *I am in a quest for freedom. In this moment I choose release. I forgive.* By the end of the month, you have forgiven seventy-seven times. It wasn't easy, but by showing mercy, you are practicing what James called "the law that gives freedom."[11]

Jesus told a story of a master who cancelled a huge debt for one of his servants. That servant, however, refused to forgive others for much smaller debts. How did the master respond? He called his servant into his office. He told him he was a wicked man, then turned him over to the authorities to be tortured. Yes, *tortured.* After Jesus told this story, he uttered a frightening sentence: "This is how my heavenly Father will treat each of you unless you forgive your brother from your heart."[12] When I refuse to release the wrongs that have been done against me, I am leading myself into a torture chamber. When I would not forgive my friend, it wasn't *he* who was suffering. I chose not to forgive, and so my heavenly Father let my soul bear the natural consequences. For many months I experienced the torturing of my own pathetic soul. The day I forgave him, heavy chains fell off of my heart. I ran out of that torture chamber as a free man.

Ask God to show you anything at all in your life that is weighing you down, suffocating your freedom, or hindering you from rising into the purposes and plans God has laid out for you. Perhaps God will give you a new perspective on your material possessions. Perhaps there is bitterness in your heart against another person, and God is calling you to release your long-held anger. Perhaps you find yourself hiding behind a false identity, and the burden of the mask you wear is weighing down the freedom of your soul. Perhaps this chapter has raised more questions than answers. Wherever you find yourself, know that God is calling you to scale mountains and run in wide-open spaces. Root yourself in Christ, allowing him to breathe his life into you and set you free from cravings that lead only to static living and emptiness. Take a step forward with your new, light feet.

CHAPTER 8

JUMP

STEPPING BEYOND THE EDGE

A s an eye surgeon, Dr. Friesen could have amassed a bank load of cash and gone straight to the top of the ladder. But he and his wife, Ruth, were a little different. We might even call them insanely free. Herb was an ophthalmologist with an imagination. For him, the ability to perform surgery to repair damaged eyes was far too precious of a skill to be wasted on petty pursuits like piling up more money in his checking account or replacing his old barbeque grill with the latest model. Herb was a humble man who chased God-sized dreams. Bent on squeezing every ounce of mileage possible from his medical skills, he was driven to perform on the creative edge.

Jesus said, "Store up for yourselves treasures in heaven, where moth and rust do not destroy, and where thieves do not break in and steal."[1] In light of this command, Herb and Ruth were brilliant investors. They were living in Afghanistan when the Soviets invaded. From an eternal perspective, this was something like dropping one's life savings into Microsoft in 1976. Instead

of running for safety, this remarkable couple made an astonishing decision. They turned their faces toward the storm. By
faith, they stepped forward into a certain risk. Before them was
an opportunity to live the life worth dying for. There, in what
might be considered the most dangerous region on the planet,
Herb and Ruth unleashed their creative talents in response to
widespread chaos and human desperation. During the conflict,
thousands of Afghans, especially children, were mutilated by
explosives. All along, Herb and Ruth were determined to be
the body of Christ, to be God's hands, live with God's heart and
respond with a tangible, visible expression of God's love. Herb
worked with others to establish and direct eye hospitals and clin-
ics for training Afghan doctors in Kabul, Mazar-e-Sharif, and
Herat. They moved with a horde of Afghan refugees to Peshawar,
Pakistan where another eye clinic was established. Before his
death, Herb trained more than thirty Afghan eye doctors. Today,
he is remembered by uncounted thousands for his gentle manner and his unrelenting passion for serving the masses.

I once asked him if he ever had any regrets about his life,
even while his medical school classmates were enjoying fabulous
retirements in the plushest golf resorts in Florida. My question
was met by a curious expression, then a big laugh. Thank good-
ness he concluded that I was cracking a joke.

Until the day he was carried up into eternity, Uncle Herb
always reminded me of another physician. It was Jesus who
walked to the front of his hometown fellowship and was handed
a scroll. He opened to a passage from Isaiah and began reading:

> *The Spirit of the Lord is on me,*
> *because he has anointed me*

> *to preach good news to the poor.*
> *He has sent me to proclaim freedom for the prisoners*
> *and recovery of sight for the blind,*
> *to release the oppressed,*
> *to proclaim the year of the Lord's favor.* [2]

Luke records that after reading these words from the parchments, Jesus sat down and began his message. The first words of his sermon were, "Today this scripture is fulfilled in your hearing." [3] It is likely that Jesus went on to explain why and how this Scripture was about to be fulfilled. He would have articulated his own dreams. Jesus shocked his own people by defying their image of what success really looks like. He publicly identified himself as a person taking action to confront the problems and the needs around him. His dreams stretched far beyond his own village, his own clan, and his own people. There were hundreds of canvases around him that he could have chosen, as there are mountains of opportunities to create around you and me even today. We all would do well to carefully think through the four conditions of human desperation that Jesus identified.

Poverty. Injustice. Blindness. Oppression.

Tomorrow morning you will rise out of bed and tomorrow night you will fall asleep. Between those two moments, more than 20,000 people will perish of extreme poverty. 10,400 children under the age of five will die of pneumonia and diarrhea. More than 1.4 billion people will survive the day on less than $1.25. Over 2.7 billion of God's image bearers will live through tomorrow without ever hearing that Jesus was crucified and rose up from the grave to redeem them from sin and set them free. Nor will they hear how precious they are in the sight of God next week, month, or year. They will age, wither away, and perish having never heard of God's love for them. The statistics, of course, could go on and on and fill up our book shelves. We all want to succeed. And yet success is largely redefined when we discover innovative ways to put our skills and talents to work on behalf of God's own dreams. We all have a measure of gifts, wealth, strengths, skills, and creative talents. From an eternal perspective, to use them only on behalf of ourselves and our own children is like investing a million bucks in Enron. In other words, we will enter eternity with virtually no treasures on the other side. Let's use a bit of imagination, take a step of faith, and strike out to explore the possibilities that God has waiting. How might we activate our own assets to create in response to the opportunities in the world around us?

When I asked my friend John what his motivation is for being a pastor, he didn't tell me he wants to grow his church or increase the tithe. He said, "There are people in our community who are living without hope. Our mission is to go out and find them, to bring the hope of Christ to them, to let them know that their Creator loves them and has moved in response to the deepest cry of their souls." John describes the broken marriages in his community. I can hear God's love in his voice when he describes the experience of carrying hope right into people's homes, helping couples identify solutions to their problems, coaching them to resolve their marital dilemmas, and helping them restore trust, intimacy, and harmony in their relationships. I was inspired by John's decision to take a huge pay cut when he walked away from his lucrative import-export business. At the time, it seemed like a certain risk. Now, though, when I see the joy in his eyes, I am reminded that there is no career that is worth standing in the way of what God calls us to.

Donny and Kaylor are committed to helping teenagers who are struggling in school. One can find junior high students hanging out at their house almost every afternoon. With their help, kids are getting up and rising to the challenges before them. Jennifer has dedicated herself to serving Indonesian children with special needs. God's love is so clearly thriving in her heart. The joy in her eyes as she interacts with children and trains teachers is inspiring to everyone around her. Beatrix bakes cookies for all the people who live in her apartment building. She takes her small children by the hand to deliver these gifts. These expressions of friendship have opened up countless opportunities to share God's love with others. Cyndi's mom devotes every Thursday to visiting a woman who has polio and can't get out of her house very often. She often takes other women along. They call that special time "Lucille's coffee hour."

My friend Kara was meeting increasing numbers of mainland Chinese immigrants in her Toronto neighborhood. Noticing that most of them had very limited English, she saw an opportunity to serve them by starting an English club. She began meeting on Wednesday evenings with a handful of Chinese women in the basement of her church. Within a month, the place was packed. Soon she began to encounter some resistance from the Ladies Missionary Society, who also met in the building on Wednesdays. The ladies were trying to pray for missionaries in China, but there was so much laughter coming from the Chinese people in the basement that they could hardly hear their own voices. Kara was told that if she wanted to continue bringing all of those people into the church, she would have to keep the noise down. Kara wasn't even fazed. Her feelings weren't hurt. She simply smiled — *release!* — had a good laugh at the irony in this looming conflict, found a practical solution, and pressed forward.

If you have what it takes to make a lot of money, then you already have what it takes to serve the world's neediest people. Why not activate your talents on behalf of the 1.1 billion people on this earth who barely survive on less than a dollar per day? Are you a writer? The ends of the earth offer the opportunity for you to write powerful, life-changing literature for translation into languages that have very few books of their own. Are you a teacher? What prevents you from teaching children in neighborhoods that most desperately need your help? Are you an attorney or a corporate executive? If you have the abilities to lead a Fortune 500 corporation, then I'd say you have what it takes to lead a team into the other side of New York, the side that is ravaged by revenge, languishing in poverty, and caught up in violence. If you have the guts to face a boardroom full of scowling faces, then I bet you have the guts to turn your face into a hurricane and keep your eyes open.

If all this feels a little heavy, don't worry. God simply asks that you focus your eyes on Jesus. Follow him, listen for his voice, and trust in his calling. He's already dreaming your dreams, and he can't wait to share them with you.

FAITH SURGE ∾

A myriad, eclectic whirl of ideas from a loud crowd of philosophers and religious teachers were creeping around, teasing the souls of the young only to leave them empty and starving for spiritual substance. Some resorted to violence. Others worshiped the past. Others tried to drown themselves in an oppressive din of religious rituals. All of them seemed to be obsessed with debating their philosophies. These elements collided to form the original context for the explosive movement that we now remember as the primal church.

Doesn't this sound familiar? In other words, history has now come full cycle. Never during these 2,000 years has our planet so closely resembled the environment where Jesus strategically chose to launch his movement. In the perfect moment in time, Jesus rose into that chaos, voicing radical words of certainty and offering himself as the one source of eternal life. He was afraid of nothing. He stood face to face with his accusers, and he did not melt away. Where others had disengaged, he came closer. Everywhere he walked, he responded to others in a way that created vision in place of blindness, hope in moments of desperation, and clarity in the midst of confusion. Some people were enraged. Some were suddenly able to see. Others were so profoundly touched by his love that they wept at his feet. None could deny that there was a fresh and compelling authority in him that artificial religion had always been powerless to display.

Jesus walked among us with improvisational freedom, exercising total authority over the weight of the world. Even before he was nailed to a cross and rose up victoriously from death, every aspect of his life demonstrated resurrection power over the gravity of death all around him. Jesus offered himself as the Redeemer, the consummate solution to every facet of our fallen world. Nothing could hold him down. His words tore through the clutter, merging confrontation with hope. His stories crashed through our dreary, desolate grind with the light of hope. He awakened a faith so pervasively transforming that it would forever change the course of human history.

Jesus preferred hanging out beyond the narrow, crumbling walls of institutional structures. He naturally gravitated toward the disenfranchised, the downtrodden, and the rejected fringe. He spent most of his time in places where streams of humanity converged upon one another. The marketplaces, watering holes, parties, weddings, and funerals offered him a natural canvas on which he could create. He was drawn to the people everyone else ran from. He responded to the desperate cries of those whom the religious elite had long ignored.

Jesus tirelessly reaffirmed his authority to give freedom. He called his disciples to recognize his own freedom at work in them. He didn't just talk about freedom. He powerfully demonstrated his creative authority at work in others. For a man named Zacchaeus, one moment with the Master was enough. For years he had been drowning in his own internal sickness. Using the luck of his position to manipulate the system, he had pilfered money from the poor and enriched himself with their coins. Jesus looked out over the crowd and called the man's name. Then he walked through the man's front door. That evening Jesus didn't transform water into wine. He didn't raise the dead, silence the waves, or cleanse anyone from leprosy. He was going after the ultimate miracle: the redemption of the human heart.

Jesus spent an evening partying with Zacchaeus. Somehow, just being with the Master was enough to awaken this man's heart and set him free from the inside out. What was it about Jesus? What did they talk about? Was it the courage and hope in his eyes? Perhaps it was the truth in his words that cut through all the shadow layers and touched Zacchaeus' soul. The result is clear. Zacchaeus was powerfully, undeniably wrenched out of his creative paralysis. He was drawn from darkness into light and set free to dream new, wider dreams. As he began imagining how he might unleash his resources to set others free, his community immediately felt the impact of his transformed heart. As Jesus watched the unfolding of freedom in his new friend, he joyfully announced that salvation had come to that house.

Jesus is calling your name. He is offering you the chance to walk in freedom. He's calling you to find your roots, your culture, your identity, and your vision in his movement. Know that in him you are set free. He has ransomed you to live and walk in the freedom of a redeemed soul. Let God's own words sink in, "The truth will set you free." "He has sent me to proclaim freedom for the prisoners." "Where the Spirit of the Lord is, there is freedom." "It is for freedom that Christ has set us free."[4] God is calling you into a way of living that rises to create, overcoming even the most towering and roaring waves of desperation and hopelessness. He is calling us into the startling realization that we are temples of the living God, housing his Spirit in our souls.

Our near future is rooted in the early church, when men, women, and children gazed steadfastly into the eyes of Christ while their bodies were mangled by growling beasts. What raging source of exultant passion and courage was bursting from within those radiant temples of God! They were the living, breathing expressions of eternity captured in finite jars of clay.

We live at a time when every shade of religion is being examined under the lights of a global arena. Frauds are being exposed. The Creator of the universe beckons people who live by faith to surge forward. As we advance into this arena, the power in our souls will be put to the test. We will not just read of Elijah and the prophets of Baal. We will stand again on Mount Carmel and find out for ourselves whether the Spirit that ignited Elijah's fire still lives. We are entering an age when living faith will explode with the rushing wind of the Spirit of God and carry us to the edge. Those who live with this faith will overcome the world.

Martin Luther King Jr. said, "A man who won't die for something is not fit to live." Where, now, do you stand? What are you willing to die for? Will you advance with the Spirit of the Living God into the most dangerous places of desperate need? The Spirit may draw you in the direction of people who need to be set free. He may even lead you to search out the loneliest person at the office and take him out for lunch. He may tell you to lay everything down in order to unleash grace into a city that has been leveled by an earthquake. He may lock you up in a dark prison cell in some barren place and throw away the key. If that's where he calls you, then be assured, there is no greater freedom than what can be found in there.

THE EDGE ∽

Not far from our city here in Indonesia lies a small island. It is the kind of place a person might imagine in dreams. Its only residents are monkeys, birds, and the occasional viper. On the far side lies a secret spot, a lagoon surrounded by the purest white sand I have ever seen. At high tide, ocean waves tumble through a hole in the cliffs, filling the lagoon with shimmering blue water. For years now, our family has gone there to pass away breezy Saturdays in paradise. Nothing that gorgeous comes easily. Getting there requires that we drive to the southern shore of our own island, then wave down a fisherman to take us in his puttering boat across the channel and drop us off. We have to jump off the boat into the water, wade to the shore, and then trek through the jungle for about two hours to get to the lagoon. We spend the morning swimming, splashing, and playing in the cool water. The kids collect shells. Our favorite spot is a majestic ridge that beckons us to climb to the edge of her wind battered cliff and gaze southward across the Indian Ocean toward Antarctica.

Standing on the precipice of that cliff gives Stephen and me the jitters. Father and son, we share a common fear of falling from high places. We cannot even crawl to the edge of that cliff without feeling vertigo. The earth beneath our feet starts to sway and spin, and we feel the urge to creep back away from the edge.

But it is only from the edge of the cliff that we see God's ocean of love, his waves of grace, and the wideness of his mercy. The edge is frightening, but the view is worth it. As I look back over my life, I see a path winding through valleys, across deserts and over mountains. At times, I've faced formidable peaks. At other times, I've stood on the edges of cliffs, looking down over a vast landscape, and not knowing how to move forward. Each of those moments is a story unto itself. They look and feel so different from the others, and yet they are also the same.

God brings us around to moment after moment where we are given another chance to plunge more deeply into him. To make the jump is to take a risk. His Spirit within us challenges our calloused old habits. As we stand facing our Creator, the world around us slows, then freezes into silence, leaving us alone under the wide-open sky and in the silence of our thoughts. We must choose. To turn away would mean continuing to exist through some half-lived, masked charade. To step more deeply into him involves tearing our souls open and being swept into his dreams.

God is always the more dangerous option.

I will take hold of your hand.

    I will keep you and will make you

    to be a covenant for the people

    and a light for the Gentiles,

to open eyes that are blind,

    to free captives from prison

    and to release from the dungeon

    those who sit in darkness.

ISAIAH 42 : 6–7

ACKNOWLEDGMENTS

I thank the Lord for Mike O'Quin, who urged me to write this book and sparred with me through the entire creative process. You are a brother and friend for life.

Being a first-time writer, I was a bit nervous about what to expect from an editor. Mercifully, God provided Angela Scheff and the team at Zondervan, who saw possibilities in this manuscript and challenged me to aim higher.

Eric Bryant, thanks for putting your reputation on the line. I will never forget it.

I am so deeply grateful for Thomas Addington, Margaret Hartzler, Wade Harlan, Ben Sustar, Jesse Chang, Luke Samoff, Larry Clement, Stephanie Myers, Katherine Douglass, and Kim Duffy, who pored through the manuscript and responded with valuable insights.

Erwin McManus, my pathfinder — for beckoning my dreams into uncharted territory.

To my teammates here in Indonesia and coworkers at Charis, thanks for being our family away from America.

To our supporters who pray without ceasing and give through Pioneers and Mustard Seed, I simply cannot express how grateful I am for your sacrifices.

My precious little ones, Katie, Josiah, and Stephen—thank you for sharing your early mornings and weekends with me and my laptop this year. Let's go ride bikes!

Most of all, thank you, Cyndi, for demonstrating every day what living faith looks like. You are my inspiration. I love and treasure you beyond words.

NOTES

CHAPTER 1: RESPOND

1. First John 5:4.
2. See John 12:32.
3. Matthew 13:14.
4. John 3:8.
5. Acts 17:28.
6. Second Samuel 22:29–30, 33–37.
7. Second Samuel 22:5–7.
8. See 2 Samuel 22:8–11.

CHAPTER 2: ENGAGE

1. Nehemiah 1:3.
2. Acts 17:16.
3. Exodus 4:10.
4. See 1 Kings 19:18.
5. Bruce Ellis Benson, "Call Forwarding: Improvising the Response to the Call of Beauty," *The Beauty of God: Theology and the Arts* (Downers Grove, IL: InterVarsity, 2007), 76.
6. Matthew 5:14–16.
7. See Matthew 10:27.
8. Matthew 10:28.
9. These images are all drawn from Isaiah 58:6–10 using both the KJV and the NIV.
10. Romans 8:19.

CHAPTER 3: ABSORB

1. Genesis 1:1–2.
2. See Genesis 32:28.
3. Genesis 1:26.
4. See Genesis 6:6; 1 Samuel 15:11; and 2 Samuel 24:16.

5. Genesis 3:13; 4:6; 6:13; 17:9; 35:1.

6. Psalm 104:30.

7. John 5:17.

8. Hebrews 13:8.

9. Isaiah 41:18–20.

10. First Corinthians 3:9.

11. See Acts 21:11.

12. H.W. Janson and Anthony F. Janson, *History of Art* (Upper Saddle River, NJ: Prentice Hall, 1997), 806.

13. Van Halen, Edward Van Halen, Alex Van Halen, Michael Anthony, David Lee Roth, "Hot For Teacher," *1984*, Warner Brothers, 1984.

14. Ralph Waldo Emerson, "Self Reliance," About.com, http://grammar. about.com/od/60essays/a/selfrelianessay.htm.

15. Matthew 11:16–17.

16. John 1:1–3.

17. John 1:4 (emphasis added).

18. Second Corinthians 4:6.

19. Ephesians 2:10.

20. See Acts 13:4–12.

21. Judges 3:10.

22. Judges 6:34.

23. Judges 11:29.

24. First Samuel 10:6.

25. Second Samuel 23:2.

26. Second Chronicles 24:20.

27. Isaiah 32:15.

28. Isaiah 42:1.

29. Isaiah 61:1.

30. Matthew 10:20.

31. Matthew 12:18.

32. Matthew 12:28.

33. Mark 1:12.

34. Mark 13:11.

35. Luke 12:12.

36. John 14:26.

37. John 15:26.

38. Acts 1:8.

39. Acts 2:4.

40. Acts 4:31.

41. Acts 13:4.

42. Acts 20:22.
43. See Exodus 31:3.
44. See Daniel 4:8−9.
45. See Judges 14:6.
46. See Joel 2:28.
47. Second Timothy 2:21.
48. See 2 Corinthians 3:18.

CHAPTER 4: AGONIZE

1. See Hebrews 11.
2. Luke 7:50; 17:19; Matthew 9:29; Mark 10:52; and Matthew 15:28.
3. Vincent van Gogh to Theo van Gogh, Nuenen, October, 1884, trans. Johanna van Gogh-Bonger, ed. Robert Harrison, 378, http://webexhibits .org/vangogh/letter/14/378.htm.
4. Vincent van Gogh to Theo van Gogh, Nuenen, October, 1884, trans. Johanna van Gogh-Bonger, ed. Robert Harrison, 378, http://webexhibits .org/vangogh/letter/14/378.htm.
5. See Mark 8:34; Luke 10:25−37; and Luke 18:18−30.
6. John 16:33 (emphasis added).
7. Second Corinthians 12:9 (emphasis added).
8. First Corinthians 2:5.
9. Zechariah 4:6.
10. See Colossians 4:18.
11. Colossians 1:9.
12. www.mustardseed.org.
13. Philippians 4:13.

CHAPTER 5: ASSIMILATE

1. Luke 6:45.
2. First John 4:19.
3. See 2 Corinthians 1:3−4.
4. Romans 15:13 (emphasis added).
5. See Luke 8:11−15.
6. Luke 8:15, NASB.
7. Matthew 23:26.
8. Mother Teresa and Jose Luis Gonzalez-Balado, *Mother Teresa: In My Own Words* (New York: Gramercy Books, 1996), 10.
9. See Matthew 7:24.
10. Don Richardson, *Eternity in Their Hearts* (Ventura, CA: Regal, 1981), 24.

11. *The Zondervan Pictorial Encyclopedia of the Bible* states that both Greek words are virtually synonymous. For example, a comparison between 2 Peter 3:5 and Hebrews 11:3 reveals that *Rhema* and *Logos* both describe God's creating word.
12. Isaiah 55:11, NKJV.
13. Hebrews 1:3.
14. Hebrews 4:12.
15. See Ephesians 6:17.
16. Colossians 1:5–6, NASB.
17. First Thessalonians 2:13, NASB.
18. Second Thessalonians 3:1, NKJV.
19. First John 2:14.
20. Jeremiah 20:9, NKJV.
21. Colossians 3:16.

CHAPTER 6: ANTICIPATE

1. Matthew 13:31–32.
2. Matthew 5:14.
3. John 1:47.
4. John 1:42 (emphasis added).
5. Luke 5:10.
6. Acts 4:13.
7. Second Corinthians 9:8.
8. Ephesians 3:20.
9. U2, "Stand Up Comedy," *No Line on the Horizon*, Interscope Records, 2009.
10. Luke 18:22.
11. Second Kings 6:17, NKJV.
12. Hebrews 11:1, NKJV.
13. See Luke 11:9.
14. Jeremiah 29:13.
15. Deuteronomy 4:29.
16. C. S. Lewis, *Prince Caspian: The Return to Narnia* (New York: Collier Books, 1951), 140.
17. Matthew 5:8.
18. See John 12:32.
19. *Vine's Expository Dictionary of Biblical Words*, s.v. "draw."
20. See John 16:13.
21. See Matthew 23:17.

CHAPTER 7: RELEASE

1. Colossians 3:23.
2. Psalm 69:3, NKJV.
3. Second Corinthians 2:4, NKJV.
4. First Corinthians 2:3–5.
5. See Acts 20:37.
6. François Mauriac, *Vipers' Tangle* (New York: Doubleday, 1957), 104.
7. Luke 12:15 (emphasis added).
8. Luke 23:34.
9. Matthew 18:21.
10. Matthew 18:22.
11. James 2:12.
12. Matthew 18:23–35.

CHAPTER 8: JUMP

1. Matthew 6:20.
2. Luke 4:18–19.
3. Luke 4:21.
4. John 8:32; Luke 4:18; 2 Corinthians 3:17; and Galatians 5:1.

AUTHOR PAUL RICHARDSON ...

schedules trips to North America, where he is available to speak in gatherings of any size. To invite him, please go to his blog at: faithactivators.com.

Share Your Thoughts

With the Author: Your comments will be forwarded to the author when you send them to *zauthor@zondervan.com*.

With Zondervan: Submit your review of this book by writing to *zreview@zondervan.com*.

Free Online Resources at
www.zondervan.com

Zondervan AuthorTracker: Be notified whenever your favorite authors publish new books, go on tour, or post an update about what's happening in their lives at www.zondervan.com/authortracker.

Daily Bible Verses and Devotions: Enrich your life with daily Bible verses or devotions that help you start every morning focused on God. Visit www.zondervan.com/newsletters.

Free Email Publications: Sign up for newsletters on Christian living, academic resources, church ministry, fiction, children's resources, and more. Visit www.zondervan.com/newsletters.

Zondervan Bible Search: Find and compare Bible passages in a variety of translations at www.zondervanbiblesearch.com.

Other Benefits: Register yourself to receive online benefits like coupons and special offers, or to participate in research.

ZONDERVAN®

ZONDERVAN.com/
AUTHORTRACKER
follow your favorite authors